Warrior

Battling infertility - staying sane while trying to conceive

Tori Day

About the Author

Tori lives with her husband and two children (one big, one little). When not working in Government communications, she enjoys being mummy, reading, writing and (trying) to stay fit.

www.toridayblog.wordpress.com

Twitter @toridaywrites

For those still in the trenches

Introduction

We all know about hoping. Hoping you get that promotion, hoping your other half has cooked dinner when you get in, hoping you might create a new life this month... Sound familiar? This book won't be of interest to everyone, but I suspect it will be of interest to a very particular group, and that's those who are TTC. If you get the acronym you most likely are, or have been, in this group. It stands for 'trying to conceive', by the way. If you're bored already, then this book probably isn't for you.

I spent two and a half years of my life struggling to manage my obsession with getting pregnant. It affected my whole life in ways I would never have anticipated. Trying to conceive, for good or bad, became my sole purpose. When I was standing in the queue in a coffee shop, my mind would be going over dates and calculations, working out the optimum time to have sex. When I was in a meeting at work, I would be arguing with myself about whether to take a pregnancy test a day earlier than I'd decided to allow myself to. On the train home, I was wondering whether I should have done that shoulder stand for an extra two minutes, as that could have been the *one thing* that made the difference between my dreams coming true and trudging on in this state of semi-existence.

The trying / struggling to conceive journey can be a lonely and isolating place. It's not easy to talk about; people don't know what to say. If you're a stressed out parent with a toddler who's causing havoc in a supermarket, you can exchange wry smiles with other parents, the older generation who've been there, or basically anybody else who happens to be around.

Being a parent is hard work, but feeling frustrated because your child won't put down the bag of sweets and move on to the shampoo aisle or being exasperated because your child has thrown their food all over the floor (again), are actually Good Problems to Have. I say this because they're relatable. You can use them to bond with others, they make good anecdotes and you know that however annoying these things are at the time, you're blessed to be experiencing them.

Infertility is a Bad Problem to Have. When you're self-consciously brushing tears from your cheeks, overcome with emotion in the nappy aisle, there's nobody there rolling their eyes with you or offering an understanding smile. When you have to leave the room because someone has announced their pregnancy and they've only been trying a couple of months, you're pulling yourself together alone in the toilets. This doesn't make an amusing anecdote over dinner with friends, later. It makes people uncomfortable. I want to change that. I want it to be okay to say 'hey, I'm struggling to get pregnant and it's tough' and for people to know what to say back.

Now, I've probably inadvertently given away the ending to my story already, so in the spirit of giving hope, let me tell you now there was a happy ending for me, and there may be one for you too.

I had a baby. The whole experience floored me, changed me irrevocably, picked me up, jumbled me around and put me down somewhere else entirely. A better place, to be absolutely clear.

There are few experiences as profound as bringing new life into the world. There are countless stories – novels, blogs, films, TV programmes – about people having babies, yet every story is unique. When it comes to your own baby, it feels like you're the only one to ever encounter it, and you are, because it's your unique experience.

The agonising months and years of waiting, hoping, waiting, fearing, dreading, waiting, hoping, waiting some more, the euphoric positive pregnancy test, the utter joy, the elation from seeing two lines on a white stick, are yours. The queasiness, the tiredness, the first flutters of movement, the gentle and then more definite kicks from inside your swollen belly are yours.

Since having my baby, the world has shifted. The love is the sort that brings you to your knees, stops you in your tracks and makes your heart feel as if it will burst. I warn you now, I do have a tendency to get a bit sentimental – I need to watch that. So, without getting too mushy, let's just say I'm eternally grateful for what I know is the most special time in my life so far.

Millions of people around the world have babies every day. It's commonplace. Lots of people struggle to get pregnant, lots of people have far more dramas and difficulties than I did and still have a happy ending, but this is my story. I want to tell it. I want to tell it to you – the woman living her life in two-weekly cycles, the woman dreading her period each month, the woman who has to avert her eyes when she sees a pregnant woman on the street or a chubby toddler in the park. You know who you are. You are me. I was you. So, if I have your attention, please read on.

Once upon a time on a rainy day in May, I got married to a 'right nice fella', as my mum would say. Fast forward a year and we were still trying to get pregnant…

Chapter 1
Trying, trying, trying

3 May 2014
Month 11

So it turns out keeping your sanity while trying to conceive is not all that easy. No one tells you that. You expect to feel excited by the hope and possibility of a pregnancy and a baby, then to smile wryly at your partner when it doesn't happen and skip on merrily with your life, none the worse and ready to try again. The reality is somewhat different.

My period is due next week and I can feel it's on its way. I didn't expect to be pregnant this month and I know it could still take a while from now, but I couldn't help feeling a twinge of disappointment and sadness. I'm irritable and suddenly tearful for no reason. It's PMT, I know it is. I KNOW it is. And yet. There's still that little voice whispering tantalisingly in my ear: what if it's early pregnancy hormones making you bad-tempered? What if the period pain is actually implantation pain and a little embryo is burrowing into the lining of your womb right now? I wish that voice would sod off. Hope is cruel. But is it even more cruel to have no hope at all?

In the attempt to stay sane, here are some thoughts to help me stay on this rollercoaster journey of indeterminate length without losing myself:

- The fact that we've been trying for a year doesn't mean there's a problem.
- Our bodies are not machines and Mother Nature does not always follow the laws of science
- I don't want conceiving to be all I think about and all I talk about. My thoughts at least are one thing I can control.
- Eighty percent of people conceive in the first year of trying and ninety-five percent in the first two years.
- Stress is the number one reason for conception not happening. Obsessively Googling baby-making topics causes stress. I am going to start Pilates.

10 May 2014

My period is here. I knew it was coming and, as usual, I'm relieved I can now stop wondering, 'What if?' For now, at least. There's a certain comfort in familiarity, even when familiarity is not the preferred option. I don't want to wallow or feel sorry for myself, but I can't help wondering, 'Why not yet?' and 'When will it be?' and 'Do we have a long road of doctors' appointments, tests, treatments and heartache in front of us?' I don't know the answers and I can't do anything to control what happens, which makes it so hard.

I can't control what happens, but an article in *Psychology Today* backs up my theory that I can control how I react to what is happening now. Apparently I can 'cognitively reappraise' my thoughts and thus change the way the situation affects me. So this means re-evaluating the situation, looking at it from a few different angles and steering my thoughts in a more neutral or even in a positive direction. That's not to say 'think more positively', which is annoying to hear and hard to do, but the simple act of considering what you're feeling and naming your emotion can take the negative power out of it.

I hate being late, for example. I often feel tension rising when I'm ready to go and meet friends or family for some social occasion and Craig is still in the bath/cooking food/in his PJs doing yoga (all real-life examples).

I'll say to him several times, 'Are you ready? We need to go in ten minutes'.

'Yes, I'll be ready.' (Carries on reading in the bath/stirring a pot/doing a cat cow.)

'OK, we need to go in five minutes.'

Then, 'We need to go *now*!'

Then, 'FINE! I'll wait in the car!'

Then I sit in the car watching the minutes tick by, craning my neck to try and see inside the kitchen and muttering, 'WHAT ON EARTH IS HE DOING??' I'm seething and my emotions are running away with me. I'm thinking, *It's not fair that I spend so much time WAITING for him. Does he not CARE? Other people will be WAITING for us too. They'll be thinking,* God, Tori and Craig are *always* late, how rude of them. *They'll start to lose respect for us and stop inviting us to do things…'*

OK, stop! I'm spiralling into an abyss.

I'm starting to be irrational and it's going to ruin the car journey, if not the whole day.

So, I can recognise I'm feeling tense and frustrated (that is, name my emotions), and I take a deep breath and think through some other points of view. *We probably won't be that late. I told him we needed to set off a bit earlier than we actually do, because I know he always leaves it until the last minute. The reason he's running late is because he was preparing dinner, so it's ready for us when we get home. People probably won't notice or care too much if we're a few minutes late, they might not be on time anyway.* All of these things are true, and I'm not getting all Pollyanna about it, just nudging myself gently into a more neutral/positive direction until everything feels a little bit better.

So, back to the matter in hand. I'm not pregnant this month, but instead of feeling sad, angry, frustrated or disappointed (or all of the above), I can consider some other points of view. *It's not so bad, because I get another month to save more money, spend more time with Craig, drink wine and eat rare steak/blue cheese/runny eggs.*

In fact, further Googling tells me habitual use of reappraisal is also linked to improved memory for emotional situations and better social functioning in terms of healthy friendships and romantic relationships. So, not only can I be OK with not being pregnant, I can have a better memory and improved friendships and marriage. Sounds pretty good to me.

(Thanks, Psychology in Action website.)

Tip #1 Control your mind (or at least your thoughts)

Cognitive reappraisal aside, I still want to maximise our chances so that conception does actually happen at some point. It's difficult to know what's the best thing to do. I'm very tempted to use the ovulation sticks again. The downside of that is, they add pressure, they make our sex life a chore and generally take their toll. But then, not being pregnant every month takes its toll too. I wonder if I should use them but not tell Craig. I would know when the right time was and could make sure we had sex, but he wouldn't know so he wouldn't feel like he 'had to'. That could work, but it would mean I would be extra tense the week before my period, waiting to see if it has worked. I'm tense anyway, though. Hmm, I might give it a go.

Oh, I wish I didn't think and analyse so much. I'm sure other people don't do this!

18 May 2014

It's our first wedding anniversary. This means we've been trying to get pregnant for nearly a year. We really should be going to the doctor. I broach the topic with Craig as we sit in the sunshine on our anniversary weekend away in the Lake District.

'Shall we book an appointment at the

doctor's when we get home? It's been a year.'

'Yes, I think we should.' Craig licks his ice-cream.

'Or should we wait a bit? I mean, maybe we should just try for longer. Having tests and waiting for results can't be much fun.'

'No, but they might find something simple is causing a problem and be able to fix it.'

I admire his optimism. I fidget on the grass, running my fingers over the pattern on my ankle from sitting in the same position too long.

'Well, there's something else I'm worried about…I'm embarrassed to tell you…'

Craig looks at me quizzically. 'What can you possibly be embarrassed to tell me?'

Still looking at my ankle. 'They'll want to do a blood test and I'm scared. I've never had one before and I'll probably faint.'

Craig raises an eyebrow. 'You can't let that stop you. This is more important.'

I look up, irritated. 'I'm not saying I'll let it stop me. Of course I'll do it anyway. I'm just saying I'm worried about it. It makes me feel limp and dizzy and panicky. I can't help it. I don't *want* to feel like that.'

'So choose not to, then.'

My irritation threatens to bubble over into anger. Then I think to myself, 'cognitive reappraisal'. That's basically what he's talking about.

'Hmm,' is my response. I was looking for some sympathy and reassurance, but my husband tells it like it is. We're both quiet, lost in our own thoughts. My phone pings, interrupting my reverie. I glance down. It's a group Facebook message from Craig's cousin and his wife. I see the words 'expecting', 'due date', 'baby'. My stomach lurches as I wrestle with my emotions. This is good news, I should be happy, but suddenly my ice-cream doesn't taste right, my insides are in turmoil. I quickly do the maths. I can't help myself. They got married in October, which means they must have only been trying for four months. Not fair, not fair! I must not become bitter. *I won't, I won't.*

Craig is shielding his eyes from the sun, popping the last bit of cornet into his mouth.

'Have you seen this message?' I ask.

'What message?'

'Charlie and Becky are having a baby.'

'Oh, that's excellent.'

I scrutinise him to see how he's really feeling. He seems pretty genuine in his response.

'It is good news,' he says more softly.

I nod. 'Yes.'

'It doesn't affect us, or our chances.'

'I know that logically, but it's like someone's saying – this is how you do it, didn't you know? You've obviously been doing something wrong.'

He holds my hand. 'We'll get there. It'll be us sending a message to family telling them our good news soon.'

I nod and put my phone away. I can't

face reading all the replies or responding myself just yet.

19 May 2014

Home from our trip. As I'm writing this, I feel how strange it is that this notebook will tell the rest of my story, but that at this moment in time I have no idea what that will be. How many more pages will I write until I can write that I'm pregnant? It could be in a few pages, it could be another year of writing and onto a new notebook. As long as we get there one day – and deep down, I believe we will. I wonder when. I wonder, I wonder! Right, enough wondering. I'm going to get on with my life today and now.

We've decided to try this month and next, then visit the doc's in July to start on the tests and make sure there are no problems. In the meantime, we might use some of our baby savings for a holiday. If Sod's Law happens and I get pregnant after we've spent some of our baby savings, I would love that Sod!

1 June 2014

I'm one week from my period and I think I could possibly be having period-like twinges, but nothing I'm a hundred percent sure of. I used the sticks without saying anything to Craig and we had sex every day through the fertile time, and a few days either side to be sure. I need to stay sane for this next week. We should have a reasonable chance, but I daren't get my hopes up. Instead I'm going to tell myself it probably won't be this month. I mean, why would it? It hasn't been for the last eleven months, and isn't doing the same thing and expecting a different result the definition of insanity? I'm sure somebody wise said that. Oh yes, a quick Google tells me it was Albert Einstein. There we go, he was wise.

2 June 2014

My period is definitely coming. I've got the usual period pain. Oh, well. That's all I have to say just now.

9 June 2014

It still feels like my period is coming, but it's not here. I'm a day late. It'll probably come tomorrow, but what if…..? I'm tempted to do a pregnancy test to check, but I'm not sure I can take the disappointment of seeing that one line mocking me again. It's like it's looking me in the eye saying, 'Well, what did you expect? Are you stupid? You don't get pregnant. Other people do, but not you.' On the other hand, if I don't do a test I risk getting my hopes up. It's hard to know what to do for the best. I genuinely want to do the best thing. I don't want to torture myself and revel in the misery. I'm home on my own tonight. Craig is in London for work and I'm meeting him there tomorrow. I could pack a test and we could do it together in the hotel room if my period isn't there yet. I think it will be, though. I could do it now. Or I could try to stop thinking about it. (Ha!) I'm going to go for a run to clear my head. I don't think I am pregnant, so I won't do a test. There.

One hour later
Month 12

Just been for a run and my period is here. All that jigging around must have helped it on its way. As usual I'm sort of resigned to it and glad my mind will be at rest for a few days.

15 June 2014

The hardest part of this journey is the lack of control. I'm used to being able to do x and have it equal y. I achieve the thing I want by planning how to do it, then doing what's required to get there. When I wanted the latest *Now* tape – those of you born in the eighties will know what I mean – I saved my pocket money for x amount of weeks and bought it. When I wanted to go to university, I studied hard for my 'A' levels and I got there. When I saw a job I wanted, I applied, prepped for the interview and…didn't always get it, but after a few attempts I'd get there. Bob's your uncle, Fanny's your aunt. BUT trying to apply that mentality to TTC – no dice. It doesn't work like that when trying to make a baby – and there's the rub. You can try as hard as you like, but if it ain't happening there isn't a great deal you can do about it. This is the crux of the issue. I know for myself, a lot of the stress and worry comes from trying to control the uncontrollable. Excuse the overused quote from the serenity prayer, but it is rather fitting here. 'Grant me the serenity to accept the things I cannot change, the courage to change the things I can, and the wisdom to know the difference.'

I can't plan when or if I'll get pregnant, but I sure as hell can plan everything around it. Perhaps it's an illusion of control, but maybe, just *maybe*, if I reassure myself I'm in the driving seat for some stuff, the bits I'm a mere passenger for will be easier to stomach.

Earlier today we were at the kitchen table huddled over the laptop, drinking cups of tea.

'Wait, stop scrolling – look at that one,' I point towards the screen, 'from Hanoi to Ho Chi Minh on an overnight train. I did an overnight train in Thailand. Ooh, and an overnight boat cruise. That sounds fun. We'd be lulled to sleep by the rocking.'

Craig clicks on the link and we both crane our necks to see more. 'That does look good,' he says.

'Yes, I wanted to go to Vietnam when I went to South East Asia with Elizabeth. That was when I met Cait on her gap year. Cait went on to Vietnam, but we had to come back for work. Stupid work.' I try to get control of the mouse. 'Does it say how many are in the group?'

Craig ignores me. He fits the stereotype of a male – he can't (or won't) multi-task. At the moment he's concentrating on reading more about the route of the trip. I tap my fingers impatiently, then take out my iPhone to bring up the same page and be in control.

'It says a maximum of twelve per group. I wonder if there would be other couples, or lots of young, single backpackers.'

Still Craig doesn't answer.

'Craig!'

'Yes, just let me do this.'

I swear this will be Craig's epitaph. *'Here lie-eth Craig. Don't bother him while he "just does this".'*

I carry on scrolling. 'We could get flights from Manchester. That's good. Plus the trip is only ten days, so not too long for Emma to stay at your mum and dad's.'

Finally Craig breaks his gaze away from the screen. He's smiling.

'It looks excellent,' he says.

I beam at him. Our plan is formed:

1. Go to the doctor's next month and start the process of finding out what's what.
2. Keep trying.
3. If it hasn't happened by Christmas, book the trip to Vietnam for January.

The best part of this plan is that each month my period arrives means we're more likely to be able to go on our trip. This will take the edge off the disappointment of not being pregnant. For now, I may have found a solution to how to stay sane while trying to conceive.

Tip #2 Make a plan, but be prepared for it to change

24 June 2014

I'm feeling very upbeat. Summer is here and the sun is shining. Craig and I had a rare weekend to ourselves as Emma went to stay at Craig's granddad's farm.

Emma is my fourteen-year-old stepdaughter. Craig was raising her by himself when we got together, and she asked if she could call me 'Mum' when we got engaged. (She was eleven at the time.) So technically I already am a mum. I love Emma dearly and I'm so grateful for her. We have a lot of fun times together. Our shopping trips and lunches out, girly nights in watching *Dirty Dancing* and eating Chinese takeaways have been a blast. But I missed the first eleven years of her life, and sadly my love for her doesn't go any way to quenching my longing for a pregnancy and a baby of my own.

Craig and I met at work. I was in my late twenties and obviously an adult, but not a 'proper grown-up'. I was living in my friend's spare room and in a perpetual cycle of boozy Saturday nights out and Sunday 'hangover days' spent lounging on the settee eating KFC and watching box sets. I had bags of leisure time and spare cash, ate out frequently, spent money on new clothes, personal grooming and many hen weekends/weddings involving long journeys and hotel stays. My point is, I had no real responsibilities and was living the life of Riley – though it was tinged with an impatience to find The One, get married and have lots of babies (well, one or two). Since I've been married and had Emma in my life, it's not just 'me' anymore and I often have a strange out-of-body experience when Emma says something like, 'What's for dinner?' (Oh, right. Yes, I need to make something, that's my responsibility.) Or else, 'Am I allowed to go to a party at my friend's house when her mum and dad are going out?' (Erm, where's the parents' handbook when you need it?)

So anyway, all of this was a roundabout way of explaining why it was so good to have a whole 'date weekend'. For me, it's like the good old days, plus a husband. Win.

Our Saturday went like this:

We did Park Run. I raced across the finish line, heart pounding, thighs burning, that familiar feeling of my breakfast working its way a bit too far up. I dry-heaved as I slowed to a walk, trying not to bump into the other finishers. I checked my Garmin – 24:53 – Yes! Smashed it! A new personal best.

We went out for lunch at the café in the park, basking in the sunshine, legs pleasingly tired from the morning's exertion. We wandered through the park swapping stories from our teenage years. We've both told them over and over, but we always find a new angle or more details to share. We went for cocktails in the evening, feeling pleasantly fuzzy around the edges, then rounded the evening off with a curry – the favourite food of both of us. More amazingly, we had good sex that wasn't focused on trying to make a baby, and everything felt relaxed and lovely. I noted and appreciated all the great things in my life. I remembered how it felt when we bought our house two years ago and how excited we were to move here. I felt happy and glad for everything I've got. I won't forget how lucky I am to have Craig and Emma, to live in a great place, have a good job and my family nearby and lots of great friends.

25 June 2014

Back down to earth today, and I've been thinking about the trip to the doc's. I've done some research on IVF. We should be eligible for funded IVF treatment if:

- I'm aged between twenty-three and thirty-nine (tick),
- We've been trying for two years (we'll see).
- Or, we've been diagnosed with a fertility problem (we'll see).

So far, so good about the eligibility. However, some local areas add further restrictions, one of them being that they won't fund treatment if either partner has any existing children. I hope that's not a rule in our area. Anyway, I'm probably jumping the gun and hopefully we won't need IVF.

The other info I found out was that waiting lists vary from six months to two years and the cost of going private is around £5k. Yikes. Might have to spend some of the savings on actually getting a baby, never mind maternity leave and all the baby-related paraphernalia. It's good to have the information, but it's a long way off. Although that point about existing children is niggling at me a bit. I wonder if the doc will know the answer to that one. Perhaps I'll ask when we go.

26 June 2014

A bit of a knock-back. The thing about not being eligible for NHS funding for treatment if one of you already has a child had been playing on my mind, so I rang the clinic from work to find out. I went into a meeting room with some papers so it'd look like I was doing 'official work stuff' if anyone glanced through the door. I got put through to a brisk and business-like woman and asked my question.

'Yes, you're right. If either partner has existing children, you're not eligible for funding for IVF through the NHS.'

'Oh.' An awkward silence follows, while I tried not to lose my composure, then I say in a wobbly voice, 'That's not quite the news I was hoping for.'

Her tone softens. 'I'm sorry there isn't more we can do for you. The whole county has these additional eligibility criteria. I can send you the policy, if you like?'

Yes, although I don't know what I'm supposed to do with it. I hang up the phone and make a beeline to the loos, head down, avoiding eye contact with anyone I pass on the way. I shut myself safely in a cubicle and have a good old cry.

So, my fears were confirmed. I don't want to sound like a spoilt child stamping my feet, but it does seem unfair. I haven't had a baby of my own, but I'm being punished for marrying someone who has. Anyway, that's the situation, let's not dwell. It's approx. £5k a pop to go private. I don't want to have to spend all our savings, but on the positive side (cognitive reappraisal), at least we'd be in control and wouldn't have to go on a long waiting list. Vietnam is still on the cards, so it's not all bad. Assuming the doc doesn't find anything wrong, we now have step four of The Plan:

1. Go to the doctor's next month and start the process of finding out what's what.
2. Keep trying.
3. If it hasn't happened by Christmas, book the trip to Vietnam for January.
4. Put an end date on trying - probably when it's been two

years - and pay for IVF.

Ooh, we could pick the date according to when we'd want the baby to be born – see, I'm getting the hang of reappraising situations and having more positive thoughts.

P.S. I got a smiley face on the ovulation stick this morning. This could all be academic. Let's hope!

29 June 2014

On my way through the train station after work, my phone rings. I juggle bags to retrieve my phone while glancing at the clock and dashing towards the platform.

'Hello, is that Tori Day?'

'Yes,' I answer, distracted.

'It's Sarah from the clinic.'

Oh. I slow down, causing the sea of people behind me to part, muttering their complaints.

'I wanted to call back to see if we could help any further.'

'OK, thank you,' I say, my interest piqued.

'I'm going to find out if there are any clinics in the region that don't have the clause about existing children in their eligibility criteria. What I'm thinking is, if there are any, you could ask your doctor to refer you there.'

'Really? Would they be able to do that?'

'Honestly, I'm not sure, but it's worth an ask.'

I'm hopeful and sceptical all at once. 'Or maybe we could register with a doctor in that area?'

'Yes, that's a possibility.'

Is it though? It seems highly unlikely a GP's practice would take us if we don't live in their area. I wonder vaguely if we could give my mum and dad's address if the practice was where they lived, but quickly dismiss the idea as it'd probably be some sort of fraud.

'Or, there could be another way…'

I stop dead in my tracks at this, making sure I don't miss anything. A woman bumps into me while she's texting. 'Sorry,' we both say at the same time.

'A doctor can refer you for funded treatment if you're an "exceptional case".'

'Oh! Are we exceptional?'

'I don't know. I just thought it was worth passing the information on.'

I thank her and hang up, mind going ten to the dozen. I make my train with seconds to spare and have to stand up, getting jostled about as we head out of the station.

I decide, on balance, it still looks unlikely that we'd get funded, but it was good of her to call and give me a fuller answer. I take my phone back out and start Googling IVF treatment abroad. I'm pretty sure it's cheaper, and who knows, maybe it's better in some way. Obviously I hope it doesn't come to this, but I'll feel better once I know what the potential options are.

3 July 2014

So, this happened today… I'd had a bit of a rough morning at work – just work stuff, nothing serious. I took a rare lunch break to unwind and enjoy the sun in the park while eating my lunch. I was halfway though my egg mayo sandwich when a girl sat down at the opposite end of the bench to me. Nothing unusual there – the bench was of ample size. Then it became clear she was upset and fighting back tears. I was dithering over whether to say something to her, when a woman about my mum's age joined her, sitting close, packet of tissues at the ready.

The girl said, 'I don't know what to do.'

The woman said. 'What does he say?'

I immediately thought, *she's pregnant*, then told myself I'm obsessed, and they could be talking about anything. But lo and behold, the conversation continued and confirmed my suspicions.

'I was on the pill…We've only been together a few months…I don't think he's ready…I don't know if I'm ready.'

All met with comforting nods and handholding from the older woman. 'You don't have to go through with it. There are options'.

I mean, I have every sympathy for the poor girl's predicament, but of all the benches in all the world…yeesh. That's all I have to say about that.

13 July 2014

Month 13

I woke with stomach cramps early this morning and padded down the hallway to the bathroom. Yep, sure enough, there was my period. I sighed and reached for the tampons, resigned. I didn't expect anything other.

We're going to the doc's on 25 July to start tests and things. I'm relieved that something is happening. Hopefully we'll soon know what we're dealing with and can look at options from there. I don't imagine we'll find out anything straightaway, and it'll no doubt be a long and drawn out process with trips to fertility clinics, but at least we've taken a small step forward.

17 July 2014

Something strange is happening. I'm starting to imagine a future for myself and Craig where we don't have (more) children and I'm thinking maybe it wouldn't be so bad after all. I'm considering the possibility that it might not happen and imagining what it would be like to have a different lifestyle from the one I'd imagined. We'd have a lot of freedom. We could have exotic holidays, even go and live in another country. We could live a happy life together. I wouldn't want to spend the rest of my life feeling like I'm missing something. I've got Craig and I'd rather have him than someone who wasn't quite right and a baby. I'll make sure he knows that.

It's a difficult time, but I'm making a vow not to go to pieces over it. No matter what happens over the next few years, I'll deal with it. I won't become bitter and I refuse to be unhappy for the rest of my life, for myself, for Craig and for Emma. I'm seeing things from a different perspective and I'm taking control. By next summer we'll have saved enough for three attempts at IVF. If that doesn't work, we'll have to accept it's not going to happen for us and we'll have to think about a different sort of life together and about what could make us happy. Emma is nearly grown up. In another four years she'll be heading off to uni. She'll have her own life, and we'll be able to suit ourselves and do something exciting.

Sometimes life doesn't go the way you planned, and maybe the thing you think you want isn't necessarily the thing that will make you happy. I like my independence, I love being with Craig. A life with just the two of us wouldn't be too shabby at all. I'm not sure if all of this is some sort of psychological self-preservation and I'm fooling myself, but I'm OK at the moment, so we'll go with it.

Chapter 2
Get the doctor in

25 July 2014

Just got back from the doctor's. Craig and I sat there in front of our busy GP, ready to bare our souls, hanging on to his every word, looking for any sort of reassurance.

'So you've been trying to conceive for just over a year? No medical problems, that you know of?'

'Yes, we've been trying for over a year, and no, there are no problems that we know about.' I shuffle in my seat. Sweat trickles down my back. I glance at the window, wondering if it would be inappropriate to ask if I could open it.

'OK, well it can take a while. There's no cause to be concerned. We can run some routine tests to check for any obvious problems.'

'A blood test?' I ask

'Yes, we'll run some blood tests to check your FSH levels on days 1 to 3 of your menstrual cycle.'

'Oh, so not now?' I'm relieved and disappointed in equal measure, having psyched myself up for it, ready to prove something to myself (and Craig).

'No, you can make an appointment with the receptionist on the way out.'

I nod.

'I'll also submit a referral for semen

analysis at the hospital. In the meantime, sir, do you want to step behind the curtain and remove your bottom half?'

I glance at Craig. His expression isn't giving anything away.

'We'll just check your testicles to make sure everything is in order.'

'Yes, OK.'

He gets up and heads over to the curtain. The doctor follows. I sit at the other side, wondering if Craig is going to have sweaty balls when the doctor feels them. It's seriously hot in here. I hear, 'If you could just hold your penis out of the way...'

'Sorry, yes.'

'There's a bit of gristle here…nothing to worry about…yep, OK. Thank you.'

The doctor re-emerges, closely followed by Craig, doing his best 'nothing to see here, everything is normal' face.

'Everything seems fine. You'll get a letter about your semen analysis procedure.' The doctor looks at me. 'Make an appointment for your blood tests and the nurse will take some swabs, then we'll go from there.'

'So, what happens after that?' I ask, eager for some sort of timetable of events.

'Depending on the results, you may be referred to a sub-fertility clinic.'

My eyebrows shoot up. They should definitely consider renaming that. 'And how quickly will this all happen?' Please God, give me my timetable.

'Well, your blood test results will take

around three to four weeks to come back. Once you've had that and Craig's semen analysis, the referral will come through. Then it should be a month or two until the clinic can fit you in.'

My heart sinks. I add up the dates – it's going to be November before we know anything at all.

Back at reception, there's a long queue of people. We join the back of it, fanning ourselves with our infertility leaflets. Sticky and irritable, we get to the front and I ask for an appointment for my blood test.

'How about 9th August?' The receptionist's fingers hover over her keyboard.

'Um, no, it needs to be when I'm on my period and it's due on the 11th.' I'm acutely aware of the people behind me in the queue trying to busy themselves, pretending they can't hear.

'I've got nothing on the 11th.'

'How about the 12th or 13th? It needs to be on day 1 to 3 of my period.'
She sighs and taps the keyboard. 'The bloods nurse is pretty busy on all of those dates. Could you wait until the month after?' My expression must give her my answer, because she carries on tapping and frowning at the screen. 'Could you come in first thing on the 13th?'

'Yes!' I'm triumphant. The receptionist looks relieved too and is already looking around me to the next person in the queue. 'Sorry…' (Why am I sorry?! I curse my Britishness.) 'I need another appointment for swabs.'

'The nurse can do that on the 13th, as

well.'

Again, acutely aware of my audience, 'I'll be on my period, though. Can she take swabs then?'

'Ah, no – we'll need another date then.' And so the rigmarole begins again.

I managed to get booked in for 25 August, which is an eternity away. Now that I've been to the doctor's, I want to crack on and know what's what. Basically, we've got the ball rolling, but it's now lots of waiting, some tests, then more waiting.

Emma was in the kitchen when I got back. She was buttering toast as I told her where we'd been and why. It went something like this:

Me: 'So, you know how we've been trying for a baby for a while now and nothing has happened?'

Emma: 'Yes.'

Me: 'Well, we've been to the doctor's so they can find out if anything's wrong. I mean, hopefully there isn't and you'll have a brother or sister one day, but I can't promise.'

Emma: 'That's OK.'

Me: 'Really?'

Emma: 'Yeah, I've managed fourteen years without one, and as much as I'd love a baby sister or brother, I like it being, me, you and Dad, so I wouldn't mind.'

Me: 'Oh.' (Articulate as ever)

I felt a rush of love for her and had to swallow a lump in my throat. I gave her a big hug and said, 'Thank you.' Sometimes she surprises me by saying exactly the right thing at the right time.

26 July 2014

Solid smiley! ☺

30 July 2014

We were at a family wedding at the weekend, which was fun, until the conversation at the table took the inevitable turn. Afterwards, Craig's sister was really nice to me.

'The family is growing by the day.' Craig's aunt nods towards the dance floor, where an assortment of toddlers and kids run around pretending to be aeroplanes and skidding on their knees. I glance around the table. We are the only childless couple here.

'I wonder who might be next,' she continues.

I try to busy myself, fiddling with my napkin, and say nothing. Craig is talking to his uncle. '– all down to the industrial revolution, that's when it began –' he's clearly oblivious to the other conversation at the table.

'Jenny and Paul have just got engaged, so maybe after they're married there'll be another one on the way.' Craig's aunt isn't letting this drop. My stomach is knotting and my heart is starting to race.

'Excuse me, I'm going to the ladies,' I

say, trying to appear bright and breezy, and not show the emotional tightrope the conversation is leading me along.

Laura's on to me. She appears in the toilets a few paces behind me and asks if I'm OK. Of course someone asking if you're OK is the equivalent of being pushed off the tightrope (in a nice way). The floodgates open. She genuinely understands, though, as she's been through it. It took her six years of trying to have her first child.

We go for a walk to get some air and she holds my hand and listens while I rant about it not being fair and how there must be something wrong, or it would have happened by now.

'It will happen, I promise. Just have trust and be patient.'

Every ounce of my soul wants to believe her, but how can she possibly know? No one can. I nod and sniff. It does make me feel better. It's good not to have to pretend for a while. After I've finished feeling sorry for myself, we hit the bar and dance the night away.

It's great to have such a lovely sister-in-law, and a huge bonus that I get all these lovely new people in my life through getting married – a big extended family. She kept telling me how much she loved me (she was a bit drunk by that point), but she said I'd made Craig himself again and seeing her brother happy made her love me. That's nice isn't it?

In other news, the two week wait has

turned into the five day wait, because I'm so in tune with my body. There's five days from when I ovulate until I start to get period pain – it should start from tomorrow or the next day, then I'll know for sure I'm not pregnant. So this is both the best and worst time. I could be pregnant. But I bet I'm not. I can't help but hope, but although it sounds bad, I wish I could not hope so I wouldn't feel the crushing disappointment again and again.

My nipples have been tingling, but I'm sure they've done that before. My boobs are also sore, but that's definitely happened before. I need to STOP THINKING ABOUT IT. We're going on holiday to Italy in two weeks. I can't wait. It'll be good to be able to have a few drinks on holiday, at least. I think Craig's brother and his wife Mickey, who we're going on holiday with, will have another baby soon. From a completely selfish point of view, I hope she's not already pregnant. I'd be worried I wouldn't be able to hide how it made me feel, and I wouldn't want any awkwardness.

Mickey's just texted me and I half-expected her message to say she was pregnant (paranoid). It didn't though – it was about what we're taking on holiday.

31 July 2014

I'm pretty sure I've had some very mild period pains. My boobs are still very tender.

1 August 2014

6.30 p.m.
No period pain to speak of. Now I'm wondering if I imagined yesterday's…

11 p.m.

I have had some period pain now. I'm too weary to be upset about it. That's all I have to say.

3 August 2014

I haven't actually had any period pain at all today or yesterday. I don't think it means anything though.

9 August 2014
Month 14

My period came early, on day 28. After all that faffing about getting an appointment for the blood test on the right day, I had to change it anyway. Luckily they could fit me in and I went yesterday.

It was another sticky day at the doctor's surgery – they really need to get air con, or at least some fans.

'So, we're taking some blood today,' the nurse says, all smiles.

'Yes, I'm a bit nervous as I haven't had a blood test before and I have a tendency to faint.'

Not missing a beat. 'No problem. You

can lie down.'

In no time at all, I am lying on the bed, staring at the standard issue NHS green wall, facing away from the nurse and the syringe she's preparing (urgh). She fastens a strap around my upper arm, and I try not to think about what's happening.

'So, how is it you've got to your age without having had blood taken?'

'Just lucky, I guess.' I'm trying to keep my breathing even. My heart is beating too fast, and I'm fighting the urge to tear my arm away and say, 'Never mind, I'm not *that* bothered about having a baby.'

Sensing my discomfort, she starts prattling on about something and nothing to keep my attention away from what's happening. And…it isn't as bad as I thought it'd be. I can hardly feel the needle at all. Before I know it, she's saying those magic words: 'All done'. She presses a piece of cotton wool into the crook of my elbow and tells me to keep the pressure on. I sit up feeling rather pleased with myself, then – uh oh. My vision blurs, a cold sweat breaks out all over my body and a wave of nausea rises. I'd got cocky and sat up too soon.

'Lie back down and I'll bring you some water,' the nurse says immediately. I lie there feeling a bit foolish. Luckily, the feeling passes fairly quickly and after a few minutes I try sitting up again, tentatively. All good. Another few minutes and I'm able to stand up, thank her and go home.

My arm felt sore last night, which made me cringe a bit. Today I have quite a big bruise, but it doesn't hurt anymore. I think I've been very brave, like a kid with a sticker at the dentist. Craig thinks I'm a bit silly and making a big deal out of it, but I'm secretly quite proud of myself. I can call for the results in a week, but we'll be on holiday then, so I'll ring when we get back.

I've been thinking more about how our lives would be if we couldn't have a baby, and I'm starting to feel more and more OK about it. I wonder if all this obsessing has been about trying to achieve the goal of getting pregnant, rather than carefully thinking through and deciding what kind of life we want to have. I've always thought I wanted to have a baby, but what if that's because you're genetically designed to want to reproduce and because it's a societal norm? Girls are traditionally raised to want to be mummies, from being encouraged to play with dolls and toy prams to wanting to emulate their own mothers. I was lucky that my mum took time off work to be with me when I was young. I have fond memories of getting paints out, plastic mats on the living-room floor, an apron with a penguin on it, of catching the bus into town to go shopping, of boiled eggs and soldiers and sardines on toast. And then later, my mum being home when I finished school. Ready to greet me in a big, cosy mummy hug and to sit down with me, showering me with love and attention, ready to hear about my day.

But unlike my mum, I wouldn't want to give up work. I like my job, I like using my mind and being busy, I like structure and routine. Do I actually want the lifestyle of a stay-at-home mum? Or do I want one where I could put my own needs and desires first? We have so much more freedom and choice than our predecessors who fought for equality, and I'm eternally grateful that they fought for us, but with freedom comes responsibility. We have to make our own choices and decisions and then live with the consequences. That's a lot of pressure. If your life was all mapped out for you, you'd do what was expected and that would be that. Although to be infertile when your sole purpose was to produce and raise kids would be a bit harsh. Think I'll take the responsibility that comes with freedom.

I've done a mind map of what our lives could be like if we didn't have (more) children. We'd have more money and more freedom and lots more opportunities to travel, try new things. I could join a book club, do some volunteering, get on in my career, be successful. It's all sounding quite appealing compared with screaming kids and crappy nappies taking up all your time, energy and money. The good thing is we already have Emma, so when we're old we'll have someone to come visit us and we'll hopefully have grandchildren.

I've just finished reading *Me Before You*, a total tearjerker. If you've seen the film which came out later, it doesn't quite capture the story in the same way. The book made me think quite a lot. If you're not familiar with it, it's about a thirty-something quadriplegic who travels to Dignitas to end his own life, as he can't bear to live his life confined to a wheelchair, unable to do the things he used to love. An older woman tells him, 'Your generation find it harder to adjust. You have all grown up expecting things to go your way almost instantaneously. You all expect to live the lives you chose.'

You expect to live the life you chose. Let's think about that for the moment. We do, and it's not OK if things don't fit our idea of what our lives should be like. It struck a chord with my situation. I realised I can adapt and live a different life from the one I expected, and it could actually be a good thing. I'd have more opportunities and options than I thought I would. I wouldn't want to go to Dignitas, anyway! Craig feels the same way and I'm wondering if we're actually starting to reconsider this whole baby thing. Didn't see that one coming.

We babysat Laura's kids today. There were greasy handprints all over the front of the glass door of our oven, bits of orange peel down the sides of the settees, smears of mud on the carpet, and what I'm pretty sure was snot on the side of the TV. It was a cacophony of noise and mess, an assault on the senses, as one of them repetitively banged a wooden spoon on the kitchen floor and the other ran around shouting, 'Can't catch me, can't catch me,' over and over and over. By the time they'd left, I had to go and sit in a quiet room and not talk to anyone for ten minutes. I genuinely wondered why I want a child so much. The only thing I can think of is that it must be different when they're your own. Having children is a lot of hard work and you don't get to sit still and just 'be'.

This last year has put a lot of pressure on us and it has been emotionally draining for me. I'm starting to question whether I actually want to go through more years of emotional turmoil, being prodded and poked by doctors and constantly waiting on appointment dates and test results. I'm not sure anymore if I want to spend all that money on treatment, having to inject myself with hormones and waiting for results. It would be quite empowering to make a decision not to do that. Leave it up to chance, or decide it's not going to happen and get on with enjoying life. Choose a different life. We'll see if this feeling sticks. Again, it could all be a defence mechanism, but it feels good now, so that's OK.

11 August 2014

I was upset yesterday morning. I gave Craig a letter explaining how I feel and how I sometimes need more time and support from him. It boils down to this: I like to talk, Craig likes to be left alone to go to the gym, read football news, do DIY. I gave him an example of how a whole day had passed without us properly talking to each other. As soon as our

TV programme had finished, he opened his laptop and I was left feeling like a spare part, with all my feelings and words mounting up inside me with no escape route.

I know struggling to conceive is hard for him too, but he deals with it very differently. He'd rather put it out of his mind and get on with something as a distraction, whereas I need to be able to share and discuss. My letter led to a heart-to-heart about our relationship and he promised to allow time for us to be together.

To remind myself that he's actually quite a reasonable sort of chap, I wrote a list of ten things I love about him *and it wasn't that hard to think of them!*

Things I love about my husband:

1. He's a brilliant dad. He's been Emma's best friend, dad and mum as she's grown up.
2. He doesn't shy away from his responsibilities.
3. He's self-aware and willing to listen (sometimes). He knows he's not perfect (as no one is), but he will listen and is able to admit when he's been wrong and apologise – something not a lot of people do.
4. He doesn't hold grudges or point score. I particularly admire this, as I'm not so good at letting things go.
5. He doesn't take himself too seriously and sometimes meets digs from me with

humour, which diffuses potential niggles.

6. He's good in social situations. I can throw him into any group situation with my friends or family and he'll be friendly/witty/kind/whatever the situation calls for.
7. He's strong and dependable.
8. He's a great chef and does most of the cooking in our house.
9. We like to do the same stuff – hobbies-wise – which always helps. It'd be tough if on a city break one of you wanted to hit the shops and the other wanted to visit endless museums and art galleries.
10. He's an actual adult male. Not like one of many boy-men I dated during my quest to find a suitable life partner.

Before you start thinking my husband is perfect, believe me I could easily write a 'Things I don't like about my husband' list – he picks his nose, is never[1] ready on time, swears like a trooper and definitely has selective hearing – but writing that sort of list wouldn't be helpful, so I won't.

It's so easy for us to take our frustrations out on each other. I've been finding

---

[1] I know many relationship gurus advise against using definitive words such as 'always/never', as they are rarely true and they put the other person on the defensive. In this case, it is true. I'm not exaggerating.

that when I'm feeling low I snap at Craig and get irritated by things that wouldn't usually bother me. I've done a bit of research on maintaining a happy marriage and found lots of analogies of relationships with piggy banks. It goes like this: every time you do or say something that results in the other person experiencing a negative feeling – snapping at them, nagging about nose-picking, etc. – it's like taking pennies out of the piggy bank. Every time you do something positive – and it can be small things, such as making your partner a meal, listening and showing understanding – it's like putting pennies in. If the piggy bank gets empty or overdrawn, you're in trouble. Like real debt, you might need a long term plan, hard work and patience to get back in the black.

My open and honest communication with Craig counts as a deposit into the piggy bank. Perhaps I could show him my list of things I love about him as another deposit, or maybe I'll save that for another day. Carefully tending to our marriage and having a good old talk has made me feel better. As Jack Johnson said, 'We're better together', and knowing it's difficult for both of us helps.

Tip #3 Look after your relationship

13 August 2014

We received the semen-testing kit in the post. The 'kit' consisted of a pot and an instruction leaflet. The instruction was pretty clear. Basically, deposit your sample, take it to the hospital.

Craig examines the pot, holding it up to the light.

'Erm, it's not very big,' he says. I roll my eyes by way of response. 'No, I mean, it might be tricky to aim and, you know, *get it all in*.'

'Oh, I see what you mean, yes.' I concede. 'Do you want me to help?

'No. I think, no. I'll do it.'

I nod in response. 'Hang on, it says here the sample has to be tested within forty-five minutes of leaving the body or the sperm will die.' I wave the leaflet at him. 'The hospital is ten miles away. We have to get there at 9 a.m., there'll be traffic, what if it takes too long?'

'Oh. Erm, perhaps we should stop in a lay-by when we're near the hospital?'

I nearly spray a mouthful of tea. 'We'd get arrested!'

'Not if we explained.'

'You really want to have that conversation with a police officer? There's a school near the hospital too. Oh no, that's just too weird.' I sit on the bed deflated. 'What about in the toilets at the hospital?'

'I'm not wanking in a toilet!'

'It's not for fun, it's for medical reasons.'

'That's worse than a lay-by.'

'It's not. At least it's private!'

'No, I'll do it at home and we'll jump straight in the car and it'll be fine.' His mind is made up.

'What if there are no parking spaces? What if we don't have change for the machine?'

'One of us can take it in and one can wait in the car.'

'OK.' I nod. 'Yes, I guess we'll sort it.'

We made it. I sat on the sample pot in the car all the way there to keep it warm. Like a hen. What a carry on. We found a parking space and I tucked the pot under my armpit while we found the right place at the hospital. Luckily someone was ready and waiting to receive it and get it tested. We can call for the results when we get back from holiday. We go tomorrow (excited). It's good timing as we won't be sitting round waiting for the results of all the tests we've had.

27 August 2014

Good news. Craig's semen test came back normal and so did my blood test. Good start to the whole process. Really glad about Craig's result, as if there had been a problem there, there's not much they can do. That's about it for testing him now – for a man, it's pretty much a case of either you're all good or you're not. Bit more complicated for me.

We had a great time in Italy and relaxed about everything. I didn't even need to use the sticks when we got back!

29 August 2014

I've woken up with the start of period pain and am feeling miserable. I'd allowed myself to hope that this month might be different, because I'd been in a different frame of mind. I'd been really relaxed on holiday, and I'd wondered if maybe the problem has been that I've been too tense and stressed thinking about it. Also, my sister Cait said her friend had a theory that the amount of years you'd been on the pill equates to the amount of months it'll take you to get pregnant. Obviously this is based on no scientific evidence whatsoever, but it happened to two of her friends. One of them had been on the pill eleven years and it took her eleven months to get pregnant; the other thirteen years/months. As I was on the pill fourteen years, I was being a bit silly and thinking perhaps this was my month. I know it's stupid and doesn't make any sense, but I guess anything that offers a bit of hope makes me cling to it.

I'm feeling a bit sorry for myself generally this morning. I have a cold that's making me feel crappy and I'm not enjoying being back at work after the holiday. I can't get into the swing, and it feels like a drag. I guess it's normal to have post-holiday blues. I'm sure it'll pass. It's my birthday soon and I think Craig might be planning a trip away, so that'll be something to look forward to. Sometimes the thought of another year or another month of being aware of my cycle then being disappointed is too much to bear. I'll have to bear it, but I don't like the fact that it's having such an effect on me. It's weird because there's still a feeling of, 'Are we sure we want to do this?' Having a baby looks kinda hard and completely changes your lifestyle. I bet everyone must have these thoughts and questions when they're trying for a baby, though. I might have more of an idea than some about what it's actually like, as I have Emma. I know what it's like to be a mum to a child aged eleven onwards. I also see our nieces and nephews regularly and am under no illusions that it's fun and nice all the time.

I'm so fed up of thinking about it. I don't know what else to write. Surely I must have been over and over it all by now.

7 September 2014
Month 15

OK, we've had the first bit of real information back after being prodded, poked and examined by the doctor. My FSH (follicle-stimulating hormone) is 8.6, a little higher than ideal. This is the hormone that helps your eggs mature in readiness for release from your ovaries. You would think a high level of the hormone would be good, but it isn't. A high FSH level means your body is having to work harder to produce more of the hormone and the reason more of the hormone is needed is either because there are fewer eggs left, or they're low quality, or both. My FSH (under 10) is still within the normal range for my age, but somewhere around 5 would have been better.

This could be why I haven't got pregnant yet, but it could just as easily not be the reason, so we're not any further on. On the plus side, the blood tests also showed that I'm not anaemic, I don't have diabetes, chlamydia or rubella, and my thyroid, liver and kidneys are all functioning well. Good to know. We have an appointment at the 'sub-fertility' clinic on 23 October, where they'll talk to us about what this means and probably do some more tests (on me).

I feel sort of OK. It's kind of good if we have a reason for our infertility and it's something we can work with. It's not too good if my eggs are not up to scratch, but I have to remember that 8.6 is still within the normal range. Apparently, you only need to be concerned if it's over 25. Good old Google. But if my eggs were the problem, IVF wouldn't necessarily be the solution, unless we got an egg donor. I don't think I'd want that, though – I'd want the baby to be biologically mine. That's sort of the point. So I'm having lots more thoughts about a life with children vs a life without. I've moved on in my mind from the incessant 'When will I get pregnant?' question, which can only be a good thing. Also, it's looking more likely with each month that passes that we'll get to go to Vietnam, which, again, is a good thing.

Oh, my period started two days ago on day 30. It's hardly worth mentioning as I'm so sure it's coming each month. So we're on month 15.

15 September 2014

After a lot of um-ing and ah-ing, I decided to tell my manager at work about our fertility issues. I'll need time off for appointments and I might not be quite myself sometimes, so it's probably best if he knows. At the end of a meeting about how to improve team working in our 'geographically dispersed' team, he asked if there was anything else we should discuss.

'Actually, there's something personal I'd like to tell you about,' I venture swallowing. My palms feel a bit sweaty.

'OK.' He stops shuffling papers and gives me his full attention.

'Well, since we got married, we've been trying for a baby.'

He smiles at me encouragingly.

'And, well, nothing has happened and it's been fifteen months, so we've been to the doctor's and have been referred for some tests.'

'Ah yes, I had some friends who tried for a baby and it didn't happen for them. In the end they got a dog.'

There was a brief silence. Seriously? This is his response? I see he's immediately realised it wasn't the right thing to say and I feel for him. He's a lovely man and is clearly a bit out of his comfort zone.

I take a breath. Let's bring it back to safer ground. 'A lot of people do have problems. I'm just letting you know, as I'll be needing some time off to go to appointments over the next few months.'

'Of course, whatever you need.'

I nod my thanks.

'You know, sometimes when you're in a restaurant, you order a meal and it takes a long time to arrive. It doesn't mean they've forgotten your order.'

I nod again, more slowly this time. I'm not sure how else to respond to the restaurant analogy. This is a new one on me. I know he's trying his best to be supportive and say the right thing, though, and that helps. I'm relieved to know there's no issues with time off and I'm not going to have to lie each time.

The next day he called me and said thanks for confiding in him and asked if he could pray for me, bless him! Being agnostic, I don't actually believe that him praying for me would make any difference, but then again I do salute magpies, so who knows? Anyway, it does mean something to him so I was touched by his offer. It shows he'd gone away and thought about it and wanted to help. Bless him again.

20 September 2014

So today wasn't awkward or embarrassing in the slightest. No, because there's nothing unusual about telling your in-laws you need them to take their granddaughter so you can have sex with their son.

Let me explain. We're staying in a hotel in the Lake District for the wedding of another of Craig's cousins tomorrow. I'm ovulating – solid smiley this morning. Emma is sharing our hotel room… you're getting the picture. We go out for dinner with Emma and Craig's mum and dad. On the way there, I casually say to Emma,

'So, do you want to sleep in our room tonight, or Nanna and Grandpa's?'

'Yours,' comes the definite reply.

'OK, well perhaps you could go visit them for a bit, like half an hour? I think Nanna would like to see you.'

Emma (giving me an odd look). 'She's seeing me now.'

Hmm. Where to go from here? Do I mortify a fourteen-year-old by telling her, her parents need to have sex, or do I mortify myself by explaining the situation to my mother-in-law and asking for her help?

I go with the latter. It goes something like this:

Me (falling into step with Mum-in-law on the walk back from the restaurant): 'Erm, this is a bit awkward, but you know we're trying for a baby? Well, I'm ovulating, so erm, well, do you think you could ask Emma to come watch TV with you for a bit or something?'

Mum-in-law: 'Right, yes.'

Me (pink-cheeked): 'Oh good, thanks, bit embarrassing, ha ha ha.' (Forced laugh.)

I don't think she was actually bothered,

though. She's quite matter-of-fact and I know she'd like another grandchild, so she's happy to support us. Needless to say, it wasn't the best sex we'd ever had, but we got the job done. If it worked this time, I guess we'll have a funny story to tell about the conception!

23 September 2014

I've had loads of the egg white type cervical mucus this month (apologies for the overshare). That's the coveted clear stretchy type – a clear sign you're ovulating. It's the perfect consistency to help the sperm travel to the egg. Isn't Mother Nature clever? I had it for six days. Usually it's only one day or even one wipe, so I'm taking that as a good sign. Maybe my body knows it's a good egg and it's making extra egg white to make sure the sperm can get there. That makes sense to me.

I'm at the time of the month where I have hope. Anything could happen until I feel that period pain. It's only a month until our hospital appointment, so I can hang on in there until then and hopefully somehow we'll be further on. I'm hoping they'll say, 'Oh yes, I see what the problem is and we can easily fix you. There you go, it should work now.' Sort of like a switch off and on again. Wishful thinking, no doubt. The appointment is at the Women and Newborn's Unit, which seems a bit cruel, but hey ho, I guess it's all the same area whether you have a bun in the oven or a sad, lonely, empty oven. I have to admit (shamefully) that

even though making me go to the Women and
Newborn's unit is inconsiderate and harsh, a
small part of me is happy to go there in case it's
the only chance I get. *Hangs head*

     I found a blog online written by an
American couple who went to an IVF clinic in
the Czech Republic. It was written from the
man's perspective, which is unusual. It had me
in tears a few times, as he described the
emotional impact on both of them – so much
yearning and trepidation at every step. I sent it
to Craig and he said he found it very useful and
informative – ha ha! I think we must have been
focusing on different parts - him on the facts,
me on the emotions. It did go into a lot of detail
and I perhaps now know more than I cared to
about pumping yourself full of hormones
through injections and by putting things up your
bum!! Who knew?? Those parts left me feeling
a bit queasy, if I'm honest, but I'll do it if I have
to. Anyway, got to go, Craig shouted that
dinner's ready. (I know, he's a keeper.)

     Oh, P.S. Had a great birthday. My
present from Craig was to do the longest zipline
in Europe. It's in North Wales, so we're going to
stay in an Airbnb there next month. Very
excited, plus it's something you can't do when
you're pregnant!

25 September 2014

     I can feel a bit of period pain. Ten days
before my period, as normal. I can't be
bothered to be upset now – it's just another

month. At least I'll be able to do the zipline and can have a few drinks when we go out for Lou's birthday this weekend. I don't think it's going to happen without any help or something putting right at the doctor's. It's been too many tries with just nothing.

Chapter 3
What does it all mean? Getting philosophical

1 October 2014

Cait and I have started a philosophy course. I picked up a flyer at the weekend which said, 'Regain your balance'. It resonated with me, so I asked Cait if she fancied it too. We went to a taster session before signing up – it was an 'unusual experience', shall we say. We had to find a little room in a dusty old community centre, and when we arrived we were the only people there. There was a man from the 'School of Philosophy' running the session. He was sitting on a chair facing the room, with me and Cait as the 'audience'. He was probably in his mid-sixties, small and birdlike, shuffling papers and clearing his throat.

We sit down and he opens with, 'Why are you here?'

I start saying, 'Well, I was handed a flyer and I liked the look of the course, so I thought we'd come along and –'

He cuts me off. 'No, I mean *why are you here*? Why are any of us here?'

'Oh, well that's a bigger question.' I sense Cait wanting to giggle. We avoid eye contact with each other so we don't lose our composure (there'd be no going back).

For the next thirty minutes he goes on to pose more questions, such as, 'What does it all mean? What is my part in this? How can I find meaning and satisfaction in life?' I'm not sure he's promising the course will give us all the answers, but despite the somewhat awkward situation, it does sound interesting. After the session, we went through to another room to meet with an existing group who are on their break, having tea and biscuits. There are flipcharts up in the room and a real motley crew of people. It's a bit like a more eclectic work meeting. The man pouring the tea has a big, round belly and some teeth missing. He's very excited to have new people here. He tells us a very long drawn out joke, the sort where you think, *Get to the point, I'm bored of listening*. He reaches the punchline; 'DEFROST THE CHICKEN!' He finds his own joke so funny we can't help but laugh, even though it's more at his contagious laughter than the joke. He has to wipe away tears of mirth, while muttering to himself, 'Defrost the chicken, deary me.'

I think Cait wondered what the earth I'd brought her to, but we decided what the hell, we'd give it a go. The first class was much better. We weren't the only ones there, for a start. There were about twelve of us in the group, a nice mix of ages and people from different walks of life. There were a couple in their eighties – hats off to them. Although there was one very amusing point when the teacher asked what made us all want to come to the course, and Martha, the elderly lady, said,
'Well, when we saw "Regain your

balance" on the flyer we thought it was an exercise class, and Gerald has a bad knee, you see.'

This was all delivered dead pan, and I don't think anyone quite knew what to say. Well, they'd done their taster session and they still came along, so they must have got something out of it!

Our teacher, Dave, is the most down-to-earth sort of bloke you'll ever meet. A bit rough and ready, and always making jokes – a far cry from the nervy, middle-class older man who ran our taster session. We were much more at ease straight away.

The first term of the course is all about wisdom, which is defined as having the knowledge to allow you to live truly and happily. Sounds pretty good, I thought. The main takeaways from the first session were thinking about being wise, and asking yourself in any given situation, 'What would a wise person do?' We talked about 'the gap' – the gap between a thing happening and your reaction to it. You can use the gap to choose how you will respond. You can also lengthen the gap, even if it's just by one or two seconds. This gives you the chance to think logically rather than jumping to an emotional reaction. I liked that, and I'm sure I can use it as and when we have new things to deal with on our fertility journey.

Other big focuses were the 'present moment' and 'becoming still'. There is only ever the present moment. Most of our time is spent dwelling on the past or imagining the future, and this is what causes worry and unhappiness. There is only ever now, and you can only be happy right now. This hit home with me, as I obviously spend a lot of time thinking about the future and what might or might not happen. This is probably stopping me from being happy now.

'Becoming still' doesn't just mean becoming physically still, but also mentally and emotionally. It's about making time to stop all those circling thoughts and activity and to be in the moment. Sounds like the first step to learning about meditation. I find it extremely difficult to stop having thoughts, even for a few seconds, so any help they can give me with this would be appreciated.

Well, I've written a whole entry on a completely separate topic to TTC, so if it's simply a distraction from my overthinking, it's worthwhile.

Tip #4 Get a hobby

6 October 2014
Month 16

I'm halfway through this notebook. I wonder what that means. Is it some significant point in our journey? Probably not. My period started yesterday on day 30. I've had quite bad period pain this month and had to take painkillers all day. I don't think that's relevant to anything.

We had a fun day/night out for Lou's

birthday yesterday. We did some dancing! It'd been a while since we'd had a good dance. There were a lot of babies and children at the meal at lunchtime. I was sitting next to a girl I hadn't met before, and I noticed her looking at the babies too. A bit naughty, as I find it frustrating when people ask me, but I asked her if she had any kids.

'Not yet,' she said 'we're thinking about trying, but not sure if now's the right time – it looks hard!'

Ah – instant friends for life!
I joined in with, 'Oh, us too. We do want a baby, but we have a nice lifestyle now – lots of holidays and mini-breaks, etc.'

This was said against a backdrop of a dad on his hands and knees picking up a rogue meatball launched by his toddler, and a mum struggling to eat her meal one-handed at an awkward angle while breastfeeding her baby. We split into two groups after the meal – the ones with kids went home and the ones without stayed for drinks and dancing, including my new babyfree bezzie. We're in the more fun group for now, at least.

Today though, I'm tired and hungover, and I'm struggling. The hardest part is not knowing if it's going to happen. I'm now estimating it's about fifty-fifty. If I knew either way, I could deal with it and convince myself that whatever the outcome, it'd be for the best. I'd make the most out of the situation and see the positives it brought, but it's the in-between that doesn't allow me to think one way or another. I'm so fed up of thinking about it, I'm quite tearful. Perhaps I need to make more of an effort to be 'present' and 'in the moment'. Easier said than done. I'm so low, I'm crying now and the ink is smudging as I write. I'm so, so weary. I want to give up and get off this rollercoaster.

11 October 2014

My low point continued today. All day at work, I could barely keep it together. I trudged through emails and phone calls, feeling wretched and hoping no one would try to engage me in small talk.

When I'm finally home, Craig looks up briefly from his laptop as I walk in the bedroom.
'Hello,' he says.
I don't reply. I just go over to the bed and flop down next to him. He carries on reading the football news. I stare at the ceiling, wishing he'd ask me if I'm OK and at the same time wishing he'd leave me alone. I am impossible. I sigh loudly. Still nothing.
'How are you?' I ask.
'I'm fine, sweetie,' he says, still scrolling.
'You're supposed to ask back,' I say tetchily.
'You don't need to wait for me to ask, just tell me.'
'You're not paying me any attention. You're never available for me to talk to.'
He closes the laptop and looks at me.

'OK, so talk to me now.'

'I don't have anything to say.'

'OK…'

'Well, nothing new. You know it all already. I just feel crap.'

He moves over to hug me, and I shrug him off, feeling stifled. He looks hurt and I immediately feel guilty. I crumple.

'I'm sorry,' I say, the familiar floodgates opening up. 'I'm so fed up of all of it. I'm sick of thinking, I'm sick of feeling, I'm sick of *being*. I want a break, but I can't have a break from my stupid self and my stupid body that won't do the simplest thing in the world.'

'I know it's hard.'

I shrug. 'You can't say anything to help. It's all been said.'

He looks a bit lost.

'I'm going to see my mum,' I announce.

'Don't go see your mum, stay here with me.'

'No, I can't. I can't bear it. I need to move and go somewhere.'

'OK, well if you think it'll help.'

Half an hour later, I rock up at my mum and dad's and collapse into her arms on the doorstep. After several cups of tea and sobbing variations of, 'It's not fair', 'Why can't I have a baby?', 'What's wrong with me?!' I calm down. I think I'll feel better for a while now.

15 October 2014

Things are good with Craig and me. We

had a date night in London while we were both there for work. Not being a London girl, I still get a buzz of excitement at being in the big city. I realised, as I was standing on the escalator coming up from the tube, warm wind whipping my hair and Craig's hand resting on my hip, that I felt lighter. As if being away from home had put a distance between us and our problems. We emerged at Piccadilly Circus into the hustle bustle of too many people trying to get this way and that.

'What do you fancy to eat?' Craig asks.

'Hmm. Chinatown is just there. We could go for a real Chinese where they sell chicken feet and stuff.'

'Yeah, OK. It'll be better than the takeaway crap at home that's full of MSG and has been watered down for the western palate.'

I roll my eyes indulgently. 'Yes, real authentic Chinese, like they eat in China.'

Ten minutes later we're seated in a cosy little place with chickens hanging in the window and a big fish tank.

'Do you think you can buy those fish to eat?' Craig asks.

I glance towards the fish tank, which has a mixture of big orange goldfish and those tiny white things with a neon blue streak running down their bodies.

'Oh yes, I'll have ten of those white ones.' I laugh and start to peruse the menu. I'm feeling buoyant, happy even, as I sip my wine and discuss the pros and cons of set menu A or set menu B with my husband. I'm lucky, I think. Right here and now, whether or not we manage to have a baby frankly doesn't seem that important.

After the meal we went to the cinema in Leicester Square to see *Gone Girl* and paid an eye-watering amount for our tickets – do you get a three course meal with that?? It was the perfect film, a gripping thriller without a baby in sight.

The next morning, heading into the office, I saw an advert on the tube for a 'fertility show'. I did a double take as I didn't know that was a thing. It made me feel sort of normal, which was nice. It's a big exhibition with IVF clinics, medics and alternative therapies like acupuncture, hypnotherapy and all sorts. They have loads of seminar sessions on everything you can imagine and plenty of things you can't – fertility yoga, anyone? I thought a lot about going, but it's in London so it would be too expensive to get there. If it was closer to home I'd definitely go. Anyway, I spent a lot of time reading about the exhibitors and seminars on the train on my way home. I watched a YouTube clip on emotional freedom techniques (EFT), where you basically tap different parts of your body to release energy blockages which are causing emotional distress. I started tapping at my face, copying the woman in the video, then remembered I was on a train and looked around shiftily to see if anyone noticed. Think I got away with it, but decided it's all a bit 'woo' for me anyway. Images of women with hessian skirts and big jewellery, smelling of essential oils and talking in calm, soothing voices spring to mind.

What did spike my interest, though, was a seminar about the 'Fertile Mind'. The seminar was all about mind-body connection and supports the theory that our mind can affect our bodies down to a cellular level, so we can almost think ourselves pregnant (or at least fertile) in a mind-over-matter sort of way. The man behind the Fertile Mind brand, Russell Davis, believes your unconscious mind can control your body and guide it to do the things you want it to. He struggled with infertility himself and finally had a son, conceived naturally, which he believes was down to a change in mind-set. It's pretty compelling stuff.

According to the Fertile Mind website, 'research has shown that the stress levels of infertile women are equivalent to women with cancer, AIDS, or heart disease. It also shows that the more distress a woman reports prior to infertility treatment, the less likely she is to conceive.'

So basically I need to chill out, relax and believe it can happen, and it might just? Sounds great in theory. I've signed up to a weekly email, so we'll see what nuggets that has in it.

17 October 2014

We came close to booking the Vietnam

trip the other day, after I'd been so upset. We wanted to do something positive and have something to look forward to. I had a phone appointment with our doctor, in case I did magically get pregnant before then, to see if it would still be safe to travel. I fully expected him to reassure me and say it's a good idea, but he didn't. The conversation went like this:

Me: 'I'd like some advice on travelling to South East Asia when pregnant. We want to book a trip and are trying for a baby, so there's a small chance we could conceive before we go.'

Him: 'I can't offer you advice.' (Well that's a blow.) 'I can only point out the pros and cons and then you can make an informed decision.' (Right…) 'There's an increased risk of DVT on long haul flights when pregnant.' (I can live with that, I'll wear flight socks and do some dancing up and down in the aisle.) 'And when you're pregnant, your immune system is weakened so you're more likely to pick up some sort of bug. Your body fighting it off could then increase the risk of miscarriage.' (Oh, well, sadly that has to be a deal breaker.)

As much as I want to book the trip, I know deep down that I'm not comfortable with that risk, however small. I'd be anxious about going and I wouldn't enjoy it in the same way. Plus, I might be feeling tired/sick. So, I think we're going to have to stick to plan A and wait until the last minute to book. I hope the prices don't go up.

It's our trip to the 'sub-fertility' clinic at

the hospital next week, which I'm excited about – well, perhaps 'eager about' is a better way of putting it. It feels like things are moving and something's happening.

23 October 2014

So, we went to our appointment at the hospital this morning, only to find out it had been cancelled. (True story.) I stood in a too-long queue, eager to get to the consultant and know what the next step on our journey would be.

When I finally get to the front, a svelte and well-groomed woman behind the desk looks at my letter.

'I'm sorry, but this appointment has been cancelled. The consultant isn't in today.'

I open my mouth to speak, and months of frustration threaten to give way to despair and anger, all directed at well-groomed, svelty woman.

All I can manage is a dangerously calm, 'What do you mean, it's cancelled?'

I hold my letter out to her, as if the fact that the date was written in black and white means it must be going ahead.

'We wrote to you, to let you know,' she says, a bit impatiently.

'I didn't get a letter.' I stand my ground. Craig puts his hand on my elbow encouraging me away. I will not be encouraged. Eventually svelty sighs and taps her keyboard, frowning at the screen.

'Take a seat in the waiting area and someone will come see you.'

I breathe out a shaky breath that I didn't realise I'd been holding. OK, well is was better than being turned away completely. A compromise, if you will.

Craig and I leave the front of the queue and sit in the reception area of the maternity unit. We watch a woman in labour come in, a wild and excited look in her eye. Her partner follows closely behind, all brisk and business-like, looking out for signs to the labour ward and steering her in the right direction. We see couples taking their new babies home with balloons and flowers, looking knackered but so happy and proud. We look at posters on the walls showing pictures of pregnant women and giving advice to pregnant women. Pregnant women. I sit there stewing, slowly getting more and more worked up at the unjustness of the situation.

After a while a different woman comes over to apologise to us, although she starts her apology with, 'We sent you a letter…' and finishes with, 'We'll send you a new appointment in the post.'

I am 'assertive', shall we say. After a brief exchange, she lets me into the office to speak to the appointment-booking woman on the phone myself, to get a new date sorted then and there. Appointment-booking woman was kind and understanding, which makes all my anger dissolve and threaten to turn into tears, but I manage to keep my composure – just – and the upshot is we have a new appointment on 13 November. So three weeks to wait. All in all, not the end of the world, but another stomach-wrenching downward dip on this emotional rollercoaster I'm stuck on.

The NHS is amazing and I'm eternally grateful to live in a country where we get free healthcare, BUT they really need to sort out their processes and how they treat their patients.

I'd been doing so well, too. The philosophy classes and the Fertile Mind emails have been making me feel 'even', if that makes sense. I'll be OK again, but it's so draining and I'm so fed up of the whole thing.

It's day 20 of my cycle right now, so I'm in the 'best/worst' time where anything is possible. I used the sticks this month, so that I'd know where I was for the hospital appointment and we had sex at the right time. I'll know in a few days, but I'm going to stay positive this month. Fertile Mind – if I believe it will happen it's more likely to become a reality. Watch this space…

2 November 2014
Month 17

My period has started. As usual, I knew it was coming a few days after I last wrote. I don't have much else to say about it. I must have already said it all.

My friend recommended I try acupuncture. She's been going for her period pain and found it works. I don't know if I could cope with the needles, though. Also, if I'm completely honest, I don't quite see how it'd work. I know people say it does and I believe them, but could it be a placebo effect when helping with other complaints. Googling hasn't yielded any satisfactory answers for me – energy flows, meridians, Qu – anyone? It definitely calls for a willing suspension of disbelief and an open mind.

9 November 2014

I've woken up feeling grumpy this morning. Craig woke me when I was fast asleep and in the middle of a dream about being chained up in a cave. The dream was courtesy of Plato. A brief explanation, in case you're wondering what on earth I'm going on about. This week's philosophy class was about the Allegory of Plato's Cave. In this allegory, Plato talks about a group of people who have spent their whole lives chained up in a cave (sad, I know). They can't move their heads to look around and they're facing a wall (not sounding much better). There's a fire behind them and a walkway where people and animals can pass by – they create shadows on the wall, which the people chained up think are real, as it's all they've ever seen. They give names to what they see, chat about it and gossip. You know – the usual. Then one day one of them breaks free from his chains. He finds his way out of the cave and into the real world. The light hurts his eyes at first and he's confused about what he sees, thinking the shadows are real and the people or objects are not. Eventually he adjusts and gets his head around what's what. He's pretty excited about his discovery (obvs) so he heads back to the cave to tell his old friends all about it. They think he's bonkers and don't believe him. The story goes, he manages to persuade one or two to come with him, but most of them decide to stay where they are, where it's familiar and they know what to expect. The ones who go with him are *philosophers*. They're open to challenging the status quo and accept that they actually know very little about the world. Perhaps this is where the phrase 'seeing the light' comes from.

It's all a bit navel-gazey, but perhaps for me it means my feelings of frustration and impatience are shadows on a wall and not reality. Perhaps I should break free from my chains and go blinking into the sunlight to see what I might be missing.

Anyway, I'm still in bed writing this and feeling grumpy about being woken up and a bit sorry for myself on the whole. Can Plato help me with that? He says, 'A wise person can retain their inner balance and poise in daily situations and when tyrants (negative emotions) come, they do not rule, but pass on by.' Basically, it's fine and completely normal to have the emotions, the trick is to not be overwhelmed by them and not allow them to influence the way you act. Oh, to be so wise.

Later

I'm a bit less grumpy after a nice cup of tea and some breakfast. I'm a bit tired as work's been busy. I'm in the midst of applying for a promotion, which is a bit stressful, but exciting. It's done a good job of taking my mind off waiting for our hospital appointment. It's on Thursday, which has actually come around quickly. Hope it gets us further along somehow, but I'm feeling quite relaxed about it. That is a surprise.

Overall, if I get promoted and we have a big adventure holiday, all of this time spent trying for a baby might not have been a bad thing after all. Things do tend to have a way of working out, and if I'd got pregnant sooner, I'd have been on maternity leave by now and missed out on applying for the promotion.

On a separate note, I've stopped drinking. Well not completely, but I'm drinking within recommended government guidelines – no more than two to three units at a time. I realised that this was a bit of advice for TTC that I'd been ignoring. I'd been of the mind-set that once I got pregnant I wouldn't be able to drink for a long time, so I might as well enjoy my childfree lifestyle now. However, alcohol could be having a negative impact on my fertility, so I've decided to cut right back to give myself the best chance. It's been about a month and I actually quite like it. I can still enjoy a glass of wine with a meal, but I never have a hangover. The last time I drank a lot and had a proper hangover was when we went out for Lou's birthday, and I cried all the next day. It's not good for my emotional wellbeing, never mind physical, so I feel positive about the change I've made.

The only time it's hard is certain social situations, usually involving Craig's friends. For example Lucas and Keira's Hallowe'en party. Their parties always continue into the wee hours and there's a LOT of alcohol involved and pressure to drink. I got round it by not going – nice and simple. Luckily I already had plans to go to Elizabeth's, so I had a legitimate excuse, but I felt a bit odd about it the next day, as I suspect Craig would have liked me to have been there. There were some friends of his there who I've never met before, and I think he would have liked to introduce me. It did go on until 6 a.m. though, and by the end there were arguments, people being sick, people crying. I'm not interested in that sort of night out any more and neither is Craig. We agreed that next time we'll both go but pre-book a taxi for midnight, so we don't get too carried away but can enjoy the early part of the evening while things are still civilised. They'll probably think we've got old and boring, but I don't care. I've always thought our culture has such an odd relationship with alcohol. You have to have a damn good reason for not joining in.

I might be being a bit hypocritical, as I certainly know what it's like to have a good old knees-up. Our reserve goes out of the window and we're emboldened to speak our minds. Social situations are lubricated, new friendships are formed and existing bonds are deepened. Drinking is a social norm. How many stories start with, 'Well, we'd all had a few...', 'I was a bit worse for wear and...', 'I'd fallen asleep on the toilet when...' Oh, just me? Never mind.

There's something in our culture that gives booze the green light with bells on. It's almost like you're a bit weird if you don't partake. I'd be the first to confess that I've been guilty of cajoling those more reluctant to joining in the fun. 'Oh go on...you can leave your car here and get a taxi, or YOU CAN STAY AT MINE!' Such fun.

But as a bona fide grown-up, I'm more confident than I was. I don't need it, and so far into this new phase, I prefer not having too much. I'm able to meet new people and hold a conversation without the prop of a few glasses of wine in me. Don't get me wrong, it still helps in certain situations. Dull work do's or any situation where lots of people are sloshed and thinking they're hilarious – although my answer to this is to avoid those scenarios wherever possible.

Interestingly, Emma hasn't shown any interest in booze so far. (I'd definitely had a few Bacardi Breezers at that age.) She has bags more confidence than I had at her age, so doesn't need booze as a prop, and in any case she's not interested. She quite reasonably says, 'I don't like the taste, I don't want to be drunk and not know what I'm doing and I don't want to damage my body'. Hard to argue with that logic. None of her friends bother yet either, so she doesn't get any pressure there.

Perhaps she's rebelling against the norm in the same way we did as teenagers, but the norm for her is to see some of the grown-ups in her life getting drunk and being a bit silly. Are we breeding a new generation of non-drinkers, or at least sensible drinkers? Maybe so, although this is based on my limited knowledge of teenagers. But I do think the lad and ladette culture of the nineties is over. Peeing in the street and throwing up in the bin; not cool anymore.

I wonder how long until it's OK not to drink because you don't fancy it. Is it other people's insecurities – wanting us to join in so they don't embarrass themselves by saying something or doing something inappropriate in front of a judge-y sober person? Or do they not want us to miss out on the fun?

I'm going out on Saturday for Laura's birthday, but I've pre-warned her I won't be drinking much. She understands anyway, as she went through the same thing. Plus it's local, so I can easily sneak off when I've had enough. The very fact that I feel the need to 'pre-warn' illustrates my point beautifully.

So, here are some suggestions on coping with pressure to drink in situations where you don't want people to think you're pregnant.

These ones will work like a charm:

- Don't go to social events where you know there will be pressure to drink. Stay in, eat chocolate and watch a film. It's cosy inside and you won't miss that much anyway.
- Go, but don't stay until the end. Get something in your glass that looks like it could be alcoholic - Shloer in a prosecco glass, or soda water with a wedge of lime and ice. Hello, fake G&T. Then slope off when everyone is approaching the wrong side of merry. You don't have to say bye, they'll be too drunk to notice. Just go, then send a text in the morning to say what a good night it was.
- Suggest an alternative. If someone invites you on a night out, say you can't, but how about going for a walk and/or pub lunch instead? Then it's perfectly acceptable not to drink.

These are a bit more risky:

- Tell them you're on antibiotics. Sometimes works, but a note of caution: know your audience. I've had this met with, 'Oh, you can still have a few. It's fine.'
- Drive. Nobody will pressure you to drink, but they might question why you chose to drive, or try to convince you to leave

the car. 'STAY AT MINE!'

- Tell them you're doing Dry January (only works in January) or Stoptober (only works in October).
- You're training for a marathon. Again, know your audience. And also, remember follow up questions might be a bit awkward if you're not actually training for a marathon.

These will only work if you're OK with blatantly lying (assuming none of them apply to you), or if you don't know the person grilling you:

- You're a recovering alcoholic.
- Every time you drink you cheat on your husband, and he's said he'll leave you if you ever drink again.
- You're taking part in a scientific experiment on the link between alcohol and psychosis.

Tip #5 - Avoid getting hassle for not drinking

Chapter 4
A whole load more tests

14 November 2014

So we finally had our hospital appointment yesterday, but before I go into that

– I got the promotion at work. Yes! Hello, middle-management level. A nice step up the corporate ladder.

On to the hospital. There wasn't actually anything new, but I'm going back for another blood test at the start of my next cycle to check my FSH levels again and to see if they've changed. The hospital confirmed 8.6 was a bit high, and from what I can gather that could be why I haven't got pregnant yet. The nurse said they consider below 8 'normal', but the doc had said below 10, so there's some discrepancy there. The nurse didn't fill me with confidence as she didn't seem to know some basic stuff, which I know from my extensive Googling.

She started by saying, 'Well your FSH is nice and high, so that's good.'

I said, 'I thought high was bad?' while actually thinking, 'You're an idiot, why are you in this job?'

She looked a bit embarrassed and checked her paperwork, then confirmed that, oh yes, high is bad (cue barely-disguised eye roll). Anyway, apparently FSH levels can vary month to month, so I'm trying not to get too hung up on it for now. Will wait and see what the next one says.

After the FSH retest, on day 7 to 11 of my cycle I will go for a test where they put dye into my womb and through my tubes to check for any blockages. I have to take an antibiotic first to prevent any infections, and they said to take painkillers, as you can get period-like cramps. They will give me a local anaesthetic in my cervix, which I've had before a few years ago, when I had my colposcopy. It wasn't bad then, so I'm not too worried. I'll probably take the full day off work when I have that one in case I'm in pain. I think after those two tests we're pretty much cut loose. We have a follow-up appointment, but I suspect there's not much else they can do for us. They won't fund IVF – and if the issue is my eggs, I'm not sure that's the best solution anyway – but I'm not sure where that leaves us. Childless, probably! Oh, she also said we should both stop drinking completely, which I didn't care for.

Me: 'Do you know it's Christmas next month?'

Her: uncomfortable smile.

She wasn't the most empathetic. I didn't trust everything she said, so I'm not going to listen. I've already cut way back, and not to be able to drink at all over Christmas – and probably make everyone think I'm pregnant in the process – is just way too sad.

6 December 2014
Month 18

I had my second blood test result back this week, and my FSH levels have gone up to 9.7. Not good news. It's definitely on the high side, from what both the doctors and a wide range of websites have said.

I have to remember that nothing is conclusive at this point and not to panic, but it does seem this could be the reason I'm not pregnant. I'm going in for my 'hysterosalpingography' on Wednesday. That's the camera and dye in tubes thing. I'm not too worried about the procedure, more about what they might find. On the one hand, if they find a blockage they are able to unblock, then that could be good news. On the other hand, they may find I have more problems than potentially diminished ovarian reserves, which can't be good. We should have a clearer picture soon, but it's so exhausting.

The customer service we've had from the NHS is absolutely appalling. (Again, I have to point out that I'm so, so grateful for our free healthcare in this country. God bless our NHS, etc., etc.) BUT (rant alert) everyone tells you different things, and no one seems to know what anyone else is doing. To actually have the blood test we went to three different places in the hospital.

The receptionist: 'Are you here to have your glucose levels checked?'
Me: 'No.'
Her: 'Are you pregnant?'
Me: 'No.'
Her: 'Then why are you here?'
Me: 'Because I'm *not* pregnant.'
Her (in a loud voice): 'Oh, infertility!'
Then she pointed me in the vague direction of somewhere which turned out to be the wrong place. Honestly, they have no sensitivity or general awareness that they are dealing with actual human beings.

It was hard to get the results, as well. I had to ring twenty-five times this week (not exaggerating) and after being put through to lots of different departments and being cut off several times and having to start again, I finally got put through to someone in the lab who read out the results to me, seemingly without understanding the implications of them. I think he actually thought I was someone internal from the hospital. When I told him my name and he realised I was the patient, he hung up quickly. Oops. He told me my LH was 6.1 and estradiol 126. I don't know what those things mean. My itchy fingers want to Google. I imagine I wasn't supposed to phone up myself. I was supposed to wait until we get invited to a follow-up appointment, where we will get all the results in one go from the consultant, and she can tell us what they mean. That does make more sense, but I don't have that kind of patience. It could be months until that appointment. If they told us clearly what to expect and when, I could go with it, but it's a myriad of conflicting advice and misinformation, and I don't have any faith things will progress without me constantly pushing and chasing. I wonder if/when we go through IVF through a private clinic, will it be much different. I sincerely hope so!

We're very close to booking our holiday for late January. We're thinking of Cuba now. We went off Vietnam as we decided it would be quite similar to where we've been before. We've been thinking of India and several places in South America, but we've finally settled on Cuba and will hopefully book in the next few days.

10 December 2014

Had my hysterosalpingography today. It wasn't too bad at all – hardly different from a smear test. The woman was so nice and understanding, which made a massive difference. I'm so tired now, I'm not actually going to write any more. I'll update later, need to sleep now. Oh, we booked Cuba!

14 December 2014

OK, it's Sunday morning and I'm feeling much more awake now. I did end up a bit sore after the procedure. It wasn't like period pain – more like an odd feeling inside that I haven't experienced before. Almost like things were a bit loose and might fall out and it hurt when I coughed. Mostly I was exhausted. I'm not sure if it was from the antibiotics, or perhaps it was just emotionally draining. They were so nice to me in the hospital, I could have burst into tears. When I got there, a kind-looking nurse who smelt of talcum powder and had smiley eyes introduced herself, then said, 'First of all, I understand. You're living your life in two-weekly cycles, it's all you can think about and you're seeing pregnant women and babies everywhere.'

It was like she could see into my soul. I

wanted to hug her, as she really did understand, unlike the rude receptionist who asked me if I was pregnant and then shouted 'infertility' at me. (Well OK, she didn't actually shout it, but she said it loud and it was mean.)

Talcum powder lady told me it had taken her two years to get pregnant, and it only happened when they decided to stop trying and renovate the house instead. She had been on the pill ten years and thought that might be why it took a while. She also thought that might be the reason why I haven't conceived yet. She wasn't overly concerned about the FSH levels and basically made me stop worrying so much. All this talk of infertility and hormone levels has made my hope of it happening naturally slowly ebb away, but we still don't know that it couldn't. She told me to stop worrying, and for some reason her advice worked – for now anyway. She also reassured me about travelling to Cuba if I was pregnant.

'If you did get a tummy bug, it'd be unlikely to cause a miscarriage. You're often sick when you're pregnant anyway. You can get a tummy bug anywhere, or you could get run over crossing the street, or the plane could crash. Stop worrying and planning everything. Relax and carry on with TTC as normal and enjoy the holiday!'

For some reason, her advice sunk in. It was a message I needed to hear and one I will try hard to remember.

In terms of the actual test, my tubes are clear, which is good news. The nurse said there was a slight shadow on the lining of my womb, which *could* be a fibroid – a sort of benign growth. She wasn't sure and needed to check the x-ray results in more detail. I might be invited to an ultrasound to check it out further. If it was a fibroid I might have to have it removed, but it shouldn't be that big a deal. So, the next thing is to wait (my favourite thing) for an appointment letter, which will either be for an ultrasound, if needed, or an appointment with the consultant, where we'll discuss all the results and talk about 'what next'.

In the meantime, it's two weeks until Christmas and six weeks until we go to Cuba. Things are going great at work. So, I'm trying hard to take the talcum powder lady's advice – stop worrying and enjoy!

18 December 2014

Well, I didn't have to wait long. I got a letter the day after I last wrote. It fluttered onto the doormat, slim and white, full of promise and fear. My stomach somersaulted with apprehension and hope as I tore at it clumsily. An invitation to an ultrasound appointment on 6 January.

This is good. It's not long to wait, and I now know what the next stage is. Waiting and not knowing are my nemeses. An ultrasound is definitely better than another blood test or more dye in my tubes, and now I can happily plan for the Next Thing. (Did I mention I love planning?) The letter says I have to drink a litre of water an hour beforehand and not wee until after the scan. They'll push down on my bladder with the scan thingy, so it can be a bit uncomfortable, but I'm sure I'll cope. Hope I don't wee myself. Apparently it's because a full bladder pushes the bits they need to see further up to the surface. It's strange – all these things I would never have thought about. Then I get to have a wee before they use a dildo cam to explore what's going on from inside.

20 December 2014

I was getting changed into my running gear this morning when my phone pinged. It was Mickey.

'We have some good news, we're having another baby! I'm only seven weeks so keep it quiet for now, but wanted you to know.'

I sank down onto the bed, one leg in my running trousers and one bare and goose-fleshed. So many thoughts went through my head. *I'm pleased for them. I'm sad it's not me. I'm a horrible person for being sad it's not me. When is it my turn? She must have been concerned about how/when to tell me, which makes me feel guilty. It's their good news. I don't want to dampen that in any way. I'm obviously not very good at getting pregnant. It's so easy for others. It's just like, let's have another baby, oh hey, now I'm pregnant. When will it be me? Will it ever be me?* I shook my head hard and pressed the heels of my hands into my eyes. I quickly texted back, 'Oh, wow, congratulations! That's great news, so excited for you ☺', and I did mean it. Then I got dressed, left the house and ran six miles, a bit faster than usual.

26 December 2014

It's Boxing Day. My period is due in six days, on New Year's Eve. I've had a few twinges of period pain, but nothing conclusive. I won't get my hopes up. I doubt I will be pregnant, but I'd kind of like to know for sure, so I don't have to worry about having a few drinks. I've been quite restrained so far, alternating between alcoholic and non-alcoholic drinks on work do's and on Christmas Day. It's not as much fun, but at least I won't get a hangover.

We're going to Craig's uncle's house soon. They have a party every Boxing Day. I'm looking forward to it, but I'm a bit anxious as well. Craig's cousin and his wife will be there with their new baby, Mickey is pregnant, and all the other couples in our generation already have babies or young children. Seriously, all of them. It's like I'm being tested constantly. I found out on Sunday that another one of Cait's friends is pregnant, after trying for two months. I made a list of all the people I know who have got pregnant during the time we've been trying and I got to fifteen. Fifteen! I realise this is verging on obsessive behaviour and was an unhelpful thing to do, but I wanted to see whether I'd just imagined lots of people had got pregnant, or whether in fact they actually had. There were also seven pregnancies in the year we were planning our wedding, when we were putting 'trying' on hold. So that's twenty-two times I've heard someone else's happy news. As much as I want to be strong and happy for other people, and as much as I know what other people do doesn't affect my situation, I am human and I do find it hard and frustrating to hear the news, every time. I'm keeping my promise to myself (and Craig) that I won't get all B&T (bitter and twisted) and I won't, but I will allow myself the occasional rant and self-indulgent cry and I won't feel bad about it. So there.

It's not just hearing the news from friends. I constantly see pregnant women and people with babies. They're everywhere. It feels like they must have been shipped in in bulk and placed in front of me wherever I go, just to taunt me. I'm aware this sounds a touch neurotic, and that a more rational explanation would be that they were always there, but that now I notice them more, in a 'confirmation bias' sort of way. I believe they're everywhere, so I notice them everywhere.

Anyway, I've found that whenever I get an attack of the green-eyed monster, instead of wishing I was them or raging inside (*don't they know how lucky they are?? why aren't they dancing around, grinning manically?*), I stop and think of them as real people with real problems just like me – only different. So, they may be pregnant, but maybe they have a nightmare boss and have been overlooked for a well-deserved promotion because of it. They may have a baby, but maybe they're also dealing with a parent with dementia, maybe they're in an abusive relationship, maybe they ate a too-spicy curry last night and are desperately seeking a toilet. It might sound a bit harsh, and obviously I don't wish these things on anyone, but it's a good leveller. Even with our friends, we don't always know everything going on in their lives. We're all struggling with something. Everyone has problems.

A friend once said to me, 'If everyone threw their problems in a pile and you saw what others were dealing with, you'd pick your own problem back out of the pile'. Maybe, maybe not. The point is, I've become so all consumed by wanting to have a baby, I can't see anything past that one thing. In my mind, having a baby must equal happiness. This isn't necessarily true. Russell Davis of the Fertile Mind would agree with me here.

Now, I'm going to get showered and ready and I'm going to have a good time at the family party. If anyone asks when we're going to have a baby, I'll smile sweetly and say, 'Soon I hope!' Other options range from the polite, but not quite true, 'We're just enjoying being married for now', to the blatantly rude, but honest, 'Bog off and mind your own business'.

Oh, Laura called me to see if I'm drinking, as she'll bring some prosecco to share if I am. I said, 'Yes!' Lovely, I feel better already now. At least we can enjoy ourselves and not have to look after a baby. Maybe I'll get smashed. Or maybe not as I will be with the in-laws. Right, game face on.

Tip #6 - Deal with envy/manage nosy friends and relatives

A bit later

I'm in the bathroom at the party, had to have a moment to myself. Everything was going fine. I've had a prosecco and have held conversations with people about their babies and children without showing any signs outwardly that it's a difficult topic for me.

Then I saw Craig's cousin's new baby.

She's five weeks old, so small and beautiful. They asked if I wanted to hold her, and I did, so I said, 'Yes.' I sat down on the settee with her in my arms, I stared at her tiny face and hands. Her eyes were open and she fixed me with a bright blue stare. I smelt her milky, baby aroma and my womb skipped a beat. Suddenly I felt all wobbly. I was hit with a tidal wave of emotion, threatening my poise. I had a pounding in my ears, I was dizzy and had to fight to stop tears coming. I looked around, but no one had noticed anything untoward. Craig was deep in conversation about football, miming a goal-scoring kick by the look of it. In that moment I felt a flash of irritation towards him. No one talked to him endlessly about their babies and pregnancies or put their newborns in his arms. He is much more able to get away from the topic, simply because he's male. I sat there oscillating between sorrow, anger and self-pity. It took every ounce of strength I had to stop myself from sobbing all over the baby. (Not socially acceptable.) I gave the baby back to her mum, saying I needed the toilet.

I very calmly said, 'I'd love to keep cuddling her, she's so lovely, but I'm actually desperate for a wee. Here you go, back to Mummy'. No one suspected a thing. Perhaps I should consider a change of career and become an actress.

So, here I am, drying my eyes and calming myself down to go re-join the party. Luckily I'm wearing waterproof mascara. Now that I've had a little cry I feel better. I'll emerge all calm and strong, head held high (like a slightly blotchy swan) and no one will know any different.

31 December 2014

New Year's Eve. The last day of the year. I have bad period pain, so I know my period will be here either today or tomorrow. I don't feel too good overall. It's been non-stop socialising, eating and drinking for the last week. I don't fancy a party tonight but we've invited people round. Oh well, I'm sure I'll be OK once it gets going.

So what will 2015 bring? Could it be a baby? A pregnancy? I hope so. If I believed in a God, I'd pray. All I can do is believe in myself and know that whatever happens I'll be OK.

Please let it be OK.

An update – half an hour later my period is here. I cried. The party was cancelled as people kept saying they couldn't come because they were sick. Guess I got my wish. Happy New Year.

3 January 2015
Month 19

A new year. It's comforting to think of a new start and new possibilities. A whole year stretching out ahead holds potential. I can't make a New Year's resolution to get pregnant, as that's outside my control, but I can make one to be happy in the moment and enjoy now.

Feeling all reflective and introspective, I've turned to my philosopher friends for advice on living wisely in 2015. Adi Shankara, an Indian philosopher from the eighth century, talks about 'the ability to discern the transient from the eternal'. We get all upset about things that come and go. They're not part of us, so we can use our reason to identify them as separate. He says, 'We're not this transient role and we're not this feeling that threatens to overwhelm us'. What I take from that is, I'm not just a woman struggling to get pregnant. This is a transient role, which will pass. My feelings of despair, fear and hope are not me. I can observe them but not become the personification of them. All a bit deep? Maybe, but I think there's something in this being able to detach yourself from events and emotions.

8 January 2015

Quite a lot to catch up on. On Tuesday I had my scan. They couldn't find much wrong at all. I sat in a big reclining chair, like at the dentist's (only different end) as a radiologist, who looked young enough to still be in school, ran a probe covered in gel across my stomach.

'All looks fine with your kidneys and pelvis,' she says. I smile nervously. She continues to move the probe back and forth, squinting at the blurry image on the screen. I wonder how she can make anything out on there and whether she's going to be able to tell me anything useful.

'OK, I'll just take a quick look inside.' She puts down the probe she was using and picks up the dildo cam. Oh God, here we go, good job I left my dignity at the door. She lifts up my paper skirt and pushes the lubed-up wand inside me. She moves it around at different angles to view my inner workings on the screen. I'm pleased and relieved to report I don't find it in the least bit arousing. I study her face, trying to work out if what she's seeing is good, bad or indifferent.

'I think I can see a fibroid.'

OK, so I do have one. I wait for her to tell me more. She's quiet as she takes a picture of it before measuring it on the screen.

She frowns and my heart slows, then she says; 'It's very small. Don't worry – it won't cause you any problems.'

'So I don't need to have it removed?'

She shakes her head. 'No, it won't affect your fertility. It's tiny and they're very common.'

'So, can you see anything else that could be stopping me getting pregnant?' I ask eagerly.

'No, everything looks fine. It's probably just One of Those Things.'

Oh great, as if that explains it all. It's good news, but I just feel more frustrated. I'm no closer to knowing why it hasn't happened. I fear I may be headed towards a vexing diagnosis of 'unexplained infertility'.

'There is one more thing to note, but it's nothing to worry about.'

'OK...?'

'Your womb has a slight dip at the top. Size and shape varies, and yours is within the normal range. I'm only mentioning it as we're going through everything with a fine tooth comb. If it were heart-shaped, with a deep dip at the top, it could prevent an embryo from attaching – and if it did attach, there wouldn't be enough space once it grew and miscarriage would likely occur at some point.'

'But mine's not heart-shaped?' I ask, alarmed.

'No, you're fine.' She smiles.

OK, so that's a win – although it doesn't feel like one. I suddenly feel my eyes prickling and blink a few times. I feel thoroughly miserable. It's supposedly good news, but I'm no closer to getting the answers I so desperately crave. Helplessness balloons in my stomach and chest like a physical presence. I want to scream and shout, but that's not socially acceptable, so I don't.

I'm not clear what happens next. I'm all adrift without my plan. I vow not to leave until I know, and ask the woman at reception. She doesn't know much about me and asks me if I'm pregnant (again!), this makes me want to punch her a little bit, but I realise it's not her fault. She tells me I'm not under a consultant, but after some tenacious pestering on my part she gives me a phone number for the secretaries. As I'm leaving I realise it's the number I already have, which I'd tried loads of times without managing to get through. Frustration wells.

Amazingly, I called the next day and got through straightaway! The consultant's secretary said my referral had been closed. (Seriously??) I pointed out I needed an appointment to discuss all the results and our options from here. She said she'd send me an appointment letter, but it wouldn't be before we go on holiday.

But then today, out of the blue, I got a text saying an appointment has been made for 22 January! That would be great, but I'm supposed to be at a team meeting in London on that day. Gah! It's the first one since I got promoted and the first one with the new team, and I can't and don't want to miss it. I was so torn. I rang and she said it was either then or 12

February. I told her my predicament and said I'd have to think about it and ring back. It wasn't a tactic, but she sighed and said, 'Give me a minute.' Then she came back on the line and offered 15 January. Yay! A date before the original appointment. *Adds 'negotiator' to growing list of potential new careers*

So, we'll be able to discuss all our results and get a full picture of where we are to date before we go to Cuba, which makes me very happy. To recap, here's everything we know so far:

- Craig's sperm is normal.
- My tubes are clear.
- Evidence suggests I'm ovulating.
- I have marginally high FSH levels.
- I have a very small fibroid.
- I have a slight dip at the top of my womb.

What I want to know next is, based on all this information, how long should we keep trying and hoping before taking action – that is, probably going down the IVF route? Obviously, if there's a reasonable chance of it happening naturally, I'd rather not go through the emotional heartache and expense of IVF, but on the other hand time could be of the essence. Tricky. Hopefully the consultant will be able to advise next week.

I'm in a good mood because Craig and I are going on a spa weekend tomorrow. I can't wait. So need some time together after the busy-ness of Christmas. (See Tip #3 Look after your relationship.) Spa treatments, prosecco in the bath, pub lunches, walks and restaurants – bliss! Plus it's only two weeks and two days until we go to Cuba. I have to say, this babyfree lifestyle is not too shabby…

15 January 2015

We had our appointment today and actually managed to see the elusive consultant this time. I was all geared up for a 'nothing terribly wrong, keep trying' sort of message, but that's not what happened.

'OK, you've been trying to conceive for twenty months and no pregnancies so far.' She peers over her glasses at me.

I nod then shake my head. 'Yes, we've been trying twenty months and I haven't got pregnant.'

'And you've *never* been pregnant?'

Yeesh, you don't have to beat me over the head with it. 'No.'

Craig leans forward in his chair, eager for information as she flicks through her notes.

'You have a heart-shaped womb,' she says.

'What? No, I have a slight dip, that's all.'

'I've reviewed your scan pictures and it looks like a heart-shaped womb to me.'

My heart starts to pound in my chest and Craig's brow creases, either in confusion or concern, or both.

'I want to book you in for an MRI scan to see how big your septum is.'

An MRI?? That sounds like a serious thing, but weirdly I feel excited that something serious is happening, like someone finally believes us that something's up.

'Then what will happen?' I ask.

'Well, depending on how big the septum is, it could stop implantation occurring and that would mean there wouldn't be enough space for a baby to grow.'

'OK. And if it is big, what then?' Please don't say it means I'll never have a baby, please, please. I struggle not to get out of my chair and shake answers out of her.

'Then we'd remove it, through a fairly simple operation.'

Oh, phew!

She goes on to explain (using a very helpful diagram) that when your womb is formed (when you're in the womb), it starts off as two tubes leading to your ovaries, then they merge in the middle to make your womb. Sometimes they don't fully separate and you end up with a join in the middle, and that's what they call a 'septum'.

This is kind of good news, as I was hoping there would be something fairly simple wrong, which they could put right. I was ready to deal with being told it was the end of the road and to keep trying, but it's not the end of the road. There's another test and maybe a solution. Dare I hope? Regardless, she recommended looking into IVF soon. She said we shouldn't delay, because of my high FSH levels. She also said to go back to the GP and see if he can refer us to a Primary Care Trust where they might fund or part fund the treatment. It's definitely worth a conversation. I'll make an appointment with our GP when we're back from holiday and see what he says. It would be good to have IVF in the UK if possible. It would be more straightforward.

Although my immediate reaction was to think this was a positive piece of news, on reflection I'm not sure. I guess it's good that we're getting some answers. Although now I'm a bit concerned that if I did get pregnant before having the MRI scan/potential operation, I'd be likely to have a miscarriage. I'm going to stop writing for now. I'm tired. I'm nearly at the end of this notebook. When I first started writing, I wondered if I'd be pregnant by the time I got to the end. Now I have my answer. I've bought a new book.

8 February 2015
Month 20

We had an amazing time in Cuba. Havana was a great city, then we headed into the countryside and stayed with a Cuban family. Their house had a porch and rocking chair, complete with a man smoking a cigar – everything you'd picture when you imagine Cuba.

I'm feeling pretty relaxed. It was so good

to get away and have some time together. There were some twinges of sadness though, particularly one evening spent walking along an idyllic beach, listening to the soothing swoosh of the waves, while the palm trees were gently swaying in the breeze and the stars were twinkling above us. It should have been perfect, but I couldn't shake the feeling the holiday was a consolation prize. You wanted a baby, but here's a perfect holiday instead.

While we were away, my mum managed to sort out the MRI date for us. She opened our post when she was feeding the cat and rang up for us. Good old Mum.

Our appointment is on Sunday, one week from now. Then the follow-up appointment with the consultant is a week after that, so not much longer to wait. In the meantime, I've been researching IVF clinics and comparing prices. We're looking at somewhere between £6k and £15k, taking into account a few variables. That's for three attempts. I have a short list of clinics in the UK and the Czech Republic. I also have a call with our GP booked to see if there's any chance of funding. I'm most likely clutching at straws, to be honest, but I want to know I've exhausted all avenues before forking out so much money.

Oh look, I'm now at the end of the book. I'll leave it there for now and do my next entry in my new book. Hopefully there will be a happy ending before the end of book two.

Ciao!

15 February 2015

It's my new notebook so I'll start all neat, like when you get a new exercise book at school. Last week was Pancake Day, also known as Shrove Tuesday to the more religious. Craig's mum invited us all to go for pancakes at the cathedral. I don't often go to church. Well actually, that's a huge understatement; hatches, matches and dispatches are the only reasons I attend a service. I don't know what it is about churches, but I always feel a bit on edge, like I'm going to do or say the wrong thing.

I didn't grow up in a religious household. My mum would say she's a Christian, but she maybe goes to church once or twice a year – Christmas and Easter, if that. There's nothing wrong with Christian values, but I struggle with the blind faith. Questions that can't be answered and answers that can't be questioned. I'm far too inquisitive to accept that's how it is just because the Bible says so. I can't overlook how *illogical* it all is – a virgin birth (Mary must have been uber-fertile, no peeing on sticks and monthly disappointment for her), rising from the dead, walking on water, poisonous apples and talking snakes. OK, I get that I'm probably taking it too literally, and perhaps it's metaphorical, but it's too much for me to swallow and just *accept*.

So when I was sitting in the cathedral, listening to the people give thanks for the food we were about to eat, it struck me that it must be such a comfort to believe in something greater than yourself, to be part of a big supportive club and to have somewhere to turn for help. It would also be easier to accept it when things didn't go your way. 'All part of God's plan.' We're all tiny specks in the universe and if a couple of us are infertile, it doesn't matter in the grand scheme of things. The human race will carry on. We'll live and die, and in a few generations no one will remember us anyway. This is all sounding a bit bleak, but I actually find it a comforting thought. It eases the pressure a bit to think of myself as less important as an individual and more important in terms of what I can bring to a bigger group, be that my friends and family, society, the universe. OK, I'm not sure I'll have that much impact on the universe, but I will on the people closest to me, and if I focus more on my responsibility to them and less on myself, that will, in turn, make me feel better, like a big boomerang of love.

In a similar way to our grandmothers and great-grandmothers having their lives mapped out for them and their roles predefined, it seems to me that religion eases some of the responsibility to make decisions for ourselves, or at least it helps us accept that when things don't work out as we want; it wasn't meant to be. When we're not pregnant another month, instead of stamping our feet at the injustice, we could smile serenely, safe in the knowledge that God had a plan for us, and we mere mortals can't do a lot to change it, so we may as well sit back and enjoy the ride, bumps an' all.

21 February 2015

I'm feeling positive about everything at the moment. I'm sure it's partly because I feel more in control of what's happening and we have a plan (my favourite thing). Since I last wrote, I've had the MRI scan and the follow-up appointment to discuss the results. The MRI was a somewhat unnerving experience. It went like this…

We're the only people in the waiting room when a young man appears, wearing a white lab coat. With his brown hair flopping into his eyes, he looks like he belongs in a 1990s' boy band. He gestures for me to follow him down a corridor.

'Did you bring a CD?' he asks over his shoulder as he leads the way.

What? I'm baffled. Did he read my mind and is now mocking me for thinking he looks like someone out of a boyband? Also, it's 2015. Who has CDs?

'A CD?'

'Yes, to listen to in the machine. It's very noisy in there and some people find it helps them relax.'

'Oh. No, I didn't. I didn't know I was supposed to.'

'Not to worry.' His eyes crinkle as he smiles. 'We have some you can choose from.'

Great. We reach the end of the corridor and he goes into a room. I loiter in the doorway, unsure whether I'm supposed to follow.

'Cher or the *Spice Girls*?' he asks, rummaging around in a drawer. Wow, it really is the 90s.

'Erm, Cher?' I say uncertainly. I can't imagine having my insides investigated while listening to '2 become 1'. Just, no.

He nods, popping the CD into a bright pink, plastic CD player. 'OK, now go into the room on your right. There's a hospital gown on the door. Put your clothes and bag in the locker and go through to the adjoining room. A nurse will show you what to do from there.'

I take the standard issue hospital gown off the back of the door and see it has the usual gap at the back. *Am I supposed to take my knickers off?* I wonder. I keep them on, favouring as much dignity as possible. I wander through the adjoining door, feeling like Alice in Wonderland, wondering what delights will await me next. Curiouser and curiouser. A tall man with short hair greets me and asks me how I'm feeling.

'OK, thanks.'

'Great. So this will take about forty-five minutes and we need you to lie as still as possible for that time. Jump up onto here.' He pats a bed and I jump aboard, lying on my back. In front of me is a big metal tube, which I guess I'm going into. He starts attaching a strap to my upper arm.

'What's that for?' I ask, alarmed.

'We need to give you something to slow down your bowel movements, so we get a clear image of your womb and fallopian tubes.'

Oh.

'OK.' I resign myself to yet another needle as he inserts it and tapes it down in the crook of my elbow.

'Wait. It's staying there, while I'm in the machine?' I'm tense.

He nods. 'Yes, you need to keep your arm still.'

As if I'd want to move it. Next thing, he puts some headphones on me and I'm being wheeled into the big metal tube. The top of it is about six inches from my face. I glance to my sides. I'm enclosed. Good job I'm not claustrophobic. An almighty noise starts up, like a hundred metal pans being dropped into a hole. I jump, then remember I'm supposed to be still. 'If I Could Turn Back Time' starts belting out in my ears, joining the racket. Oh great, that makes it all better. I sigh and concentrate on staying still, trying not to think about the needle in my arm and the metal-bashing noises.

All in all, it wasn't your average morning out.

Anyway, onto the important part – the results. It turns out I don't have a septum after all, but a bit more of a dip than they initially thought. It's known as an 'arcuate uterus'. They don't think this should affect fertility. Craig was disappointed they hadn't found anything more conclusive that could easily be treated. I thought I'd feel the same way, but I'm strangely calm about the whole thing. They want to do one more test to be sure things are as they appear (a camera in my womb, known as a hysteroscopy). If this test confirms their thinking, the advice will be to keep trying, and then to have IVF when it's been two years. I feel fine about it all. I've been in touch with the clinic in the Czech Republic and that's what we want to go for. I like the idea of getting away from work and everyday hassles and it being the two of us in the relaxed environment. We'd need to go for ten days and there are some lovely apartments on Airbnb. Plus Jet2 fly there, so the travel and accommodation for the trip only adds on around £500. All in all, it should cost around £3k. If this first attempt doesn't work, they give you a discount on the second, and if you have embryos left over from the first attempt, you only need to go back for two days. I'm actually quite excited about it. They have a fifty percent success rate for positive pregnancy tests. You have to be careful with this statistic, as some clinics only count live births as a success, so they would quote a lower success rate, but since I've never been pregnant, if they managed to achieve this with me, it would be a massive step forward.

I know this could and probably will change, but right now I'm happy and contented with life in general and not too worried about what may or may not be. My philosophy classes are paying off. I will do my best to stay in this state of mind.

5 March 2015
Month 21

I'm still feeling fine. Really fine. I'm on my period and it's OK because I've worked out (with a bit of help from my Fertile Mind friend Russell) that my happiness doesn't depend on whether I get pregnant. I'm happy right now. According to Russell, 'Our thinking tells us we need to control life, that our wellbeing is dependent on certain circumstances.' It's easy to think I'll be happy *when* or *if*, but our happiness is not dependent on external factors. If it were, when would we ever have enough to be happy? When we owned a big house? Got that promotion at work? Had a baby?? This makes me think of Don Draper's answer to, 'What is happiness?' '*The moment before you need more happiness.*' If we base our happiness on acquiring more and more stuff – if happiness is the temporary high we get from shiny new things bought to fill a void – then of course he's right. What a legend.

To be truly happy and free we need to step away from this thinking. Our sense of well-being comes from within. Well-being is actually our default position. Young kids are happy – they're born that way. We all are. It's our thinking (and perhaps partly our increasingly capitalist society) which makes us believe we need lots of extra things in order to be fulfilled.

It's not easy, but if I can manage to think only about what's happening right now, then I have no problems. The problems lie with the past and with a possible future which doesn't exist yet. (Mind – blown.)

Tip #7 - get Russell Davis of the Fertile Mind in your life – or at least subscribe to his emails

15 March 2015

It's Mother's Day. It's not sad for me, though. I still mainly consider the day as being about my own mum. Plus Emma gets me cards, and I've already had my first Mother's Day – in 2012. Emma had stayed over at her friend's house, and when Craig and I picked her up in the morning she jumped into the car, all smiles, and proudly presented me with a pink envelope covered in hand-drawn hearts and the word 'Mum', the letters oversized, nearly filling the envelope from top to bottom. I was moved as I looked at the strangeness of the word on an envelope addressed to me. I knew it was a new era. I was a mum ahead of when I expected to be and without ever having had a baby. My thoughts, even then, quickly turned to how we'd have a baby when we got married and how good it'd be for Emma to have a sister or brother.

16 March 2015

I had my hysteroscopy on Thursday and it hurt! They put a small camera through my cervix and into my womb. Camera + cervix = ouch. Things are not supposed to go through your cervix that way. It felt like an intense period pain. I was a bit panicked as I hadn't been expecting it to hurt. The nurse was giving me a guided tour of my womb on the screen, but I couldn't concentrate because I was trying to stop myself jumping off the bed. Luckily it only took a few minutes before she confirmed that I do have an 'arcuate uterus'. She had put lots of cold water inside me to help get the camera in. When I stood up afterwards, it all poured out, loads of it, like a long cold wee. It went all down my legs and all over the floor in a big puddle. I laughed nervously and said, 'Erm, is that supposed to happen?'

The nurse, nonplussed, handed me a sanitary towel. I had a paper sheet around my middle and my 'bottom half' clothes were behind a curtain at least five steps away. There was nothing for it. I wedged the pad between my legs and waddled back behind the curtain to get dressed. When I got there the pad was soaked through, so I couldn't use it. Ridiculously, given my predicament, I was far too British and felt too cheeky asking for another, so I put my knickers on and jolly well got on with it. 'It' being a rather damp car journey home. Stiff upper lip, and all that.

So, I'm glad the test confirmed what we thought. I'm fairly certain we now know everything we need to know before having IVF. I have a long medical form to fill out for the clinic. I plan to take it with me to the appointment next month to get all the info I can from the consultant. The nurse who did my hysteroscopy said I have a 'tortuous' entry route into my cervix. Yikes! Apparently it's not a problem, but it would be useful for the person doing IVF to know this in advance, so I need to make sure all the info is transferred to the Czech clinic.

17 March 2015

I'm in a hospital bed with a big round belly, my hands stroking it lovingly.

'You're not pregnant,' a mean-looking nurse is saying. She's holding up a negative pregnancy test. The bump dissolves under my hands and I'm left rubbing my flat stomach. Of course I'm not, I'm thinking, how silly of me. My work phone is ringing and I suddenly remember I'm supposed to be on the way to a meeting. I rush for the train and it's just leaving the platform. Someone is holding the door open. I can make it. I run alongside the train and leap on, the doors sliding shut behind me. But my bag is trapped, and needles start spilling out of it onto the tracks.

'She's a junkie,' a voice in the distance says.

'No, no, I'm not. I'm having IVF – to have a baby,' I say, to anyone who'll listen to me. I have to get my bag. I have to get to work. I look at the time and the hands are racing round my watch-face too fast. I'm late, I'm not going to make it.

A doctor walks down the train carriage. 'Tickets, please.'

Everyone is showing him positive pregnancy tests, rows and rows of women with big bumps. He reaches me.

'I don't have a ticket. I'm not pregnant, but I'm going to have IVF.'

He shakes his head. 'You'll never be pregnant, get off at the next stop.'

'Sweetie, SWEETIE!'

I jolt awake. Craig is shaking me. I'm disorientated as the train and the needles and pregnancy tests fade away. I'm wet with sweat, my hair plastered to the back of my neck.

'Oh.' I had a bad dream. My throat is burning and my head aches. I think I'm coming down with something.

'It's OK.' Craig puts his arm around me as I fall back into a fitful sleep.

Chapter 5
Options

21 March 2015

I'm feeling a bit down today. Not sure what's changed, but the familiar feelings of weariness and sadness have crept in. Nothing specific is wrong, but I suppose it's inevitable that I'll be a bit up and down, so I'm not going to dwell on it. I'll keep on keeping on and hopefully I'll feel better soon.

We're going out for a curry tonight for Lisa's birthday. She doesn't know we're coming. Her other half has arranged it as a surprise, so I'm looking forward to it and I'm sure I'll be fine once I get out. Lisa and I have been friends since we were seven. I moved primary schools at that age as the secondary schools in the area were going downhill fast and my mum wanted me to be able to get into a good one. At the time I was traumatised. I'd loved my old school and I'd had lots of friends. I reaped the benefits in the end, though, so it all worked out. Cheers, Mum. Anyway, I digress. Because I was so upset, my mum made contact with the other mums at the new school – God knows how, as there was no Facebook in those days – and she set up a playdate for me and Lisa at the beginning of the summer holidays. As there were then six long weeks until we'd meet again, our mums decided we should stay in touch and write to each other. Writing letters over the summer holidays is not much fun for a seven-year-old. Conversations in our house would go along the lines of, 'You need to write a letter to Lisa', 'I don't want to, I don't like her', and similarly in Lisa's house. But amazingly, after a rocky start, where we saw each other as an unwanted burden, we became friends for life. Lisa knows all the ins and outs of my fertility journey and I imagine so does her other half (she has many positive traits, but discretion is not one of them), so it'll be nice to be around someone I don't need to put on a show for. Hell, we'll probably end up discussing the ins and outs (excuse the pun, I know – cringe) of trying to conceive over dinner.

On that – I'm at the end of my fertile window for the month. We've been having sex, but it's taking its toll. Craig's getting fed up of having to do it on demand, which I completely understand. I don't particularly want to do it either, but it's a bit easier for me. I don't have to do a great deal – just lie down or bend over. I do have some romantic notion that a baby would be more likely to be made from passionate love-making rather than a mechanical function, but that's not something you can force, sadly. I know people talk about having a baby ruining your sex life, but it turns out trying for a baby can do that all by itself.

I've had lots of egg white this month – once again, apologies for the overshare – so maybe it's a good egg this month. I can't allow myself to get my hopes up, though. I don't think it will work now without any medical intervention.

I've booked tickets to a 'Routes to Parenthood' exhibition. It's a bit like that one in London, but much closer to home, so that's brilliant. I hope we don't see anyone we know, although if we did, they'd have their own reasons for being there, so I guess that'd be OK. They have IVF clinics from abroad exhibiting. I couldn't see our Czech one on the list, which is a shame, but there's some from Norway and Greece, so it'll be interesting to speak to them. I'm also keen to speak to some alternative therapists such as acupuncturists, Chinese medicine practisers, fertility masseurs, etc. All in all, it makes me feel like I'm *doing something.*

Oh, we booked our family holiday for May half-term. All inclusive, which my inner snob is not usually keen on (visions of Benidorm-style booze-fuelled karaoke sessions spring to mind), but it makes it easier with Emma and it's cheap, so I'm sure I can park inner snob and embrace inner free-cocktail drinker and ice-cream eater. Not too much of a hardship.

24 March 2015

This is new. I'm writing while on the train to London. I had a low point last night, which is why I felt the need to bring this book with me. I started to get period pains. For some reason I'd had in my head (again) that maybe this month would be different. Because I'd been feeling genuinely more relaxed about the whole thing, I hoped it might make a difference. I imagined myself saying things like, 'Oh, as soon as we decided to have IVF, I got pregnant and we didn't need it!' *Ha ha ha, how lovely.* I never learn. Why do I let myself hope? I started crying and couldn't stop for ages. Craig was comforting, but I'm so sick of it all. I've been writing for a year and trying for nearly two. It's so long, I'm boring myself with the same thoughts and feelings, but I can't stop having them. I'm strapped to a rollercoaster and every time I think I'm on a straight section, or a gentle ride around admiring the scenery, I plummet down into sadly familiar depths of despair and misery.

I wonder if the fact that the philosophy class has finished has contributed to how I'm feeling. It's only finished for Easter, not forever. I did some studying over the weekend to see if I could find anything to help. According to Swami Vivekananda, almost all of our suffering is caused by us not having the power of detachment. We need to learn how to detach our mind at a moment's notice and direct it towards something else. Doing this means we're in control and actively choosing what we think about as well as choosing what we're not thinking about. Hmm, I have a way to go.

Vivekananda says, 'To me, the very essence of education is the concentration of the mind, not the collection of facts. If I had to do my education again, I would develop the power of concentration and detachment, and with a perfect instrument, collect facts at will.'

And the key to developing a perfect instrument: meditation. Something I've been resisting as I can't do it, and also, if I'm perfectly honest, it makes me feel a bit silly. We do a sort of mini meditation at the beginning of each philosophy class, which they call the 'exercise' (of the mind, not body – exercising the body is much easier, and personally I don't feel half as silly doing it). Meditation is OK in class, because everyone is doing the same thing and it's only for a few minutes. Anyway, I decide to bite the bullet and give it a go at home. If the power of detachment is the key to staying sane, it's worth a shot.

I find a meditation track on YouTube and tell Craig not to disturb me, then I go into the bedroom and lie down on the bed with my headphones in.

It goes like this:

Soothing voice - *Relax your body, feel the weight of your feet on the floor.* (Oh, my feet are not on the floor. Should they be on the floor? I sit up on the edge of the bed and put them on the floor. Right, now concentrate. I mean, relax.) *Pay attention to your breathing, feel the tension ebbing away* (OK, I can do this), *be aware of your body, feel the weight of your buttocks pressing down onto your seat* (snigger – God, am so immature), *relax your neck, relax your jaw, your eyes* (at eyes, I involuntarily peek through my near-closed lids and see the washing basket looking rather full. I must get to that after. Damn it, I'm not supposed to be thinking about the washing. I'm going to lie down again. That was more comfortable). *Breathe in and out and with each breath out, let your thoughts float away on a pink cloud.* (I try to visualise a pink cloud carrying all my negative TTC thoughts away. Off you pop, I don't want you. Wait, was that the door? It'll be Emma coming home from her friend's house. Is she going to come up? No, sounds like she's gone into the living room. OK. I wonder what we'll have for dinner. No, back to relaxing. What's the soothing voice saying?) *As you breathe, you feel your mind emptying of thoughts.* (Do I? Is my mind now empty? No, it can't be as I'm thinking this. Maybe we could have fajitas for dinner. Argh, stop it. Stop thinking.) *As occasional thoughts pass through your mind, observe them, then let them float by.* (Oh, well that sounds better. I visualise a chicken fajita floating by on a pink cloud. Gah, that's not what the soothing voice meant. Oh, now there's some music. I lie still and listen to it, controlling my breathing, and it is quite nice to do nothing for a while, but I can't help wondering how long I have to lie there before I can get up and put the washing on. I don't think I've quite mastered the art of meditation.

Further research tells me I'm not the only one to struggle with meditation and that the same state (a clear mind) is achieved during certain activities which produce a 'state of flow'. We can be in a state of flow while playing sport, doing something creative or simply going for a walk in nature. I realise when I'm writing in this notebook I'm 'flowing'. I'm

completely focused on what I'm doing –
concentrating, while being detached from
anything else going on around me. I'm also in
this state when I'm reading a good book and
when I'm running. I'm not sure my mind is the
perfect instrument Mr Vivekananda talks about,
but I do feel a bit better. It's hard to stay
positive all the time, so it's fine to allow myself
the odd wobble. If I can keep in mind that it's
only months until we try IVF and sort of accept
that getting pregnant probably won't happen
before then – but at the same time keep trying,
just in case – then maybe I'll be OK.

When I got my period pains last night,
literally a few days after my fertile window
ended, I realised how tuned in to my body I am.
It's like I can tell what's happening inside at any
point, which in turn made me realise it won't be
any different once I've had IVF. I'll probably
know a few days after the embryo is transferred
whether it's taken. It'll be so hard to bear going
through all that if I know straightaway it hasn't
worked. It'd be devastating, don't get me
wrong, but not forever. It's going to be a very
difficult time, but whatever happens, Craig and I
will be OK and as long as I've got that, I can
cope with it. Plus, it may work!

3 April 2015
Month 22

My period started yesterday. Month 22 I
didn't think I'd still be writing and trying a year
from when I started this. I hoped it would just

happen. Of course, I still hope that now, but I don't think it will. Not in a negative way, but it hasn't worked in twenty-two months – twenty-two tries, so it's not reasonable to expect that it will work on the twenty-third or twenty-fourth attempt without changing anything. Albert Einstein might back me up here – well, if he were still around (and if I knew him) – but still. If I was doing something at work and had tried and failed twenty-two times, I'd give up and go home. Realistically, IVF is probably our only hope, so we just keep trooping on before paying for the help. Three more months, three more tries – April, May and June. Then I'll start the process of getting ready to be implanted in August. It's going to be an emotional time, whatever the outcome. Please, please let it work. Just please.

4 April 2015

I've been asking myself, 'What would a wise person do?' I know that doing some exercise, going for a run, going to the gym, going to a fitness class makes me feel better. I also know that when I'm down, I can't be bothered and then I feel worse, and it's a downward spiral. It takes a bit of tough (self) love to give yourself a kick up the bum to get out of the door – that's the hardest bit, then everything feels a bit better.

I considered this as I pounded the pavements, pink-cheeked with fresh air and with endorphins pumping round my body. The state of meditative 'flow' is one thing to be achieved during exercise, but there's more. Research from the University of Vermont tells us that twenty minutes of exercise can improve our mood for up to twelve hours *and,* according to Happify.com, exercise has the most powerful effect when we're in a bad mood. I can believe it. It doesn't have to be running, if that ain't your bag – a walk in the fresh air can have the same effect. I'm now basking in a post-exercise glow, limbs pleasingly tired, mind clear from my circling negative thoughts. Physical activity = healthy mind (and body too obviously, but that's a whole other topic).

Tip #8 Exercise (can be combined with Tip #4 Get a hobby)

24 April 2015

I haven't written for a while and quite a lot has happened. (No, I'm not pregnant.) I'm on the train to London again as I write. The fields somewhere near Grantham are whizzing by and drops of rain are hitting the window, then sliding along and making stripy patterns. There's a man at the table opposite me, trying to sound very busy and important by having loud conversations on his ever-ringing phone, saying things like, 'Let's bring Phil into the loop when we touch base next week', and 'I think with some cross fertilisation of ideas, we can identify some quick wins'. What is it about the corporate world that makes us all sound ridiculous? It's like we have to adopt a different language to speak to each other. Clearly we wouldn't sound half as professional if we spoke plain English. Anyway, I digress. The two things I have to update on are:

- We went to the fertility exhibition.
- I tried acupuncture.

We'll start with the first. It was last week, at a big conference centre. There were speakers and exhibitors from different IVF clinics, etc. There was a man from a Greek clinic talking about IVF abroad and what to look out for. He recommended doing a recce of the clinic before flying out for treatment. I can see why this would be beneficial, but it's not that practical time- and cost-wise. It hasn't put me off the Czech Republic idea necessarily, but it has made me consider it all a bit more. One of the things that attracted me was the idea of Craig and me getting away – slipping away quietly and being all relaxed together. So, I thought if we did stay in the UK, we could stay in a cottage for a couple of days while we have the treatment.

We found out loads and may have had a change of plan. There's a clinic in Manchester that offers various 'deals'. The one we were looking at was, you pay for three attempts upfront for around £11k, and if you haven't had a baby at the end of it, you get a seventy percent refund. It's a gamble, because if the first time worked, we'd have spent significantly more than if we paid for one attempt, but if it worked on the third time or didn't work at all, then we'd be quids in. I hate having to think about having a baby in these terms, but we're going to have to pay and it ain't cheap, so we need to think through the most cost effective option.

They have another offer which involves paying for two attempts for around £7k, which is a forty percent discount, but this also includes as many goes as it takes to use any frozen embryos. So, if you had three frozen on the first round and four on the second, you'd end up with nine attempts in total, all included in the cost. But again, if it worked the first time round, it means we'd have paid more than we needed.

The other deal, and the one we're most seriously considering, is their 'egg share' programme. Basically, if I'm willing to donate half my eggs from the IVF cycle to another woman, it would cost us £1,350 for the treatment, then £1,000 for any frozen transfers. So we could have three fresh cycles for £4,050, if we shared the eggs every time, or one fresh and two frozen for £3,350. Controversial? Tempting? Yes. And yes.

We went for a coffee straight after the exhibition, heads swimming with information, feeling bewildered.

'So, we could pay for three attempts. That'd take the pressure off,' I say, flicking through a leaflet.

'But we might not need three attempts.'

'No, well that's the point – it's a gamble. Or we could pay for two…oh, I don't know.'

'Well, the good thing is, we have options.' I imagine Craig entering our options on a spreadsheet and creating a formula to arrive at the right answer. He likes a good head-based decision, arrived at through logic and rationality.

'I could share my eggs,' I say. 'That'd save us a bundle.'

'Tempting, but you'd have to be comfortable with it.'

'I know. I don't know if I am. When the woman first said it, I was like, *Wait – what? Not sure about that!* But I'd like to think about it properly. I mean, maybe it'd be a really good thing to be able to help someone else.'

'It's probably the best thing you could ever do for someone else.'

'No pressure, then!' I put my chai latte down a bit firmly and some of it sloshes over the edge. I grab the leaflets quickly to save them from getting soggy and Craig mops the liquid up with his serviette.

'Of course there's no pressure. It's completely your choice and I'm with you whatever you decide.' He's very reasonable sometimes.

'What if someone knocked on our door in eighteen years, saying they're my son or daughter?'

'What if they did?'

I shrug. 'I don't know. That doesn't usually happen to women, does it? Men could have kids they don't know about, but not usually women. I suppose it's not the worst thing that could happen...'

Craig raises his eyebrows. 'Give it some thought. It is tempting.'

'I will have to mull it over, but I could do it. They'd have been through the same as us, and probably worse, to get to the point of looking for an egg donor, so if I could offer someone else hope and maybe even a baby, perhaps I should...?'

I turn it over and over as I watch the buildings zip by through the car window on our journey home. Could I? Could I do that? I remember watching an old episode of *Friends* where Joey donates sperm for cash. At the time, I thought he was crazy. Did he not realise he could have lots of kids out there? Now, I think it depends if you consider a biological link enough to make a child 'yours'. Emma is mine and she's not genetically mine. This baby would belong to another family, to a woman who'd yearned for a baby for a long time.

A few days later, I woke up and thought, 'Yes, let's explore this further.' I filled out a very long medical form, including questions about my great-aunt's ingrowing toenail in 1984 (not really, but you get the idea).So far, I meet the criteria for egg sharing. The next step is to have a blood test to check my 'anti-mullerian hormone' (AMH) levels. That's a way of checking my ovarian reserve – in layman's terms, how many eggs I have left. Females are born with around 500,000 eggs and that's a finite stock. We lose one every month when we have a period, and the rest get old, wither and eventually, by the time we hit menopause, die. Not like a male who cooks up a fresh batch of sperm every two to three days. So, to be eligible my AMH has to be above twelve, which would indicate I have a healthy supply of eggs left. They also do a urine test to check for nicotine, which is obviously fine. So if me/my eggs are eligible, I'll have to make the final decision about whether I want to go ahead. I'm about ninety percent yes, but I realise it's A Big Thing, and don't want to rush into it. They give you a counsellor as part of the process, which sounds good. If I go ahead, they will give me the normal medication and everything will work in exactly the same way, apart from when they retrieve my eggs. Half will be mine to keep and will be fertilised by Craig's sperm, and half will be given to another woman to be fertilised by her partner's sperm.

I've discovered that they have to collect a minimum of eight eggs in order to share them, in which case we'd get four each. So if there were seven eggs, I'd keep them all, at no extra cost to us and no further obligation. If there are eight or more eggs, and the figure is an odd number, they are shared and I get the extra one. After the eggs are put with the sperm, we wait to see how many are fertilised and develop into embryos. They say it doesn't necessarily lower your chance of success as they only insert one embryo anyway. I guess it would mean fewer embryos to freeze, but all in all I'm thinking it might be the most attractive option.

The train is coming in to London now and loud man is wrapping up his call and shuffling papers. I'll have to update you on acupuncture later!

26 April 2015

So, the acupuncture debacle. I'd had a busy and stressful day at work. I won't go into all the detail, but suffice it to say I probably wasn't in the best place when I arrived. I'd rushed to get there and had lots of things swirling around my mind. There was a bit of a false start, as I was in rushing mode. I got buzzed into the building and directed where to go, so I dashed up the stairs and opened a door, only to see a woman lying on the bed with needles sticking out of her - eek! I made my apologies and made a hasty retreat to the 'waiting area', which was in fact a lone chair outside the door. Needless to say, I was already feeling a bit pink-cheeked when a mumsy-type woman in her mid-sixties poked her head round the door and invited me in.

It all started innocently enough, with a few questions about why I was there, then she quickly got to the crux of the matter and started asking very blunt questions about my sex life and how often we were at it. (I'm paraphrasing.) I'm not usually a prude. Perhaps it was her mum-like qualities, but I found myself wanting to leave and have a nice sit down with a cup of tea and a biscuit. I swallowed my discomfort and told her we had sex every other day during my fertile window. She said that we should do it regularly throughout the month, rather than just the fertile time, in a condescending teacher-like tone. I explained that we don't want to and she gave me a look which was either disapproving or pitying, I'm not sure which. Either way, it put me on the defensive.

Without further ado, she asked me to lie down on the bed and she got the needles out. I immediately tensed up and had to brace myself, like I do when I have one of my now regular blood tests.

She saw my reaction and said, 'Don't worry, this is relaxing.' She put the first needle in my shin, near my ankle. Urgh. There's no fatty tissue there and I couldn't help imagining it scraping my bone or something equally horrifying. I could feel it go in, but it didn't hurt and once it was in I couldn't tell it was there anymore, but I was aware of it and didn't like it one bit. Suddenly, it all felt horribly wrong. I knew then that whatever hopeful, clutching-at-straws naivety had brought me here, having needles stuck in me was never going to be relaxing. Tears started to sting at the back on my eyes and I knew there was no going back. I was a fully-grown woman, lying on a table with a needle sticking out of my ankle, sobbing. It was, frankly, a bit embarrassing for us both.

A bit alarmed, mumsy woman asked, 'Oh, are you upset about not being able to have a baby?' Er, yes?! Then she tried to placate me with tired platitudes like, 'You're still young, plenty of time to have a baby'. It made me want to stab her in the ankle with one of her needles. The floodgates opened, and in the end I had to make my apologies, for the second time in ten minutes, and leave.

All in all, not my best afternoon. So thinking philosophically – I didn't win, so what did I learn?

- I don't like needles (knew that already).
- I don't like discussing my sex life with strangers.
- Acupuncture is not for me.

In all seriousness though, at least I've now tried it and can rule it out. If I don't believe sticking needles in yourself can help you get pregnant – and I don't, not really (IVF needles discounted) – then the only benefit to it is that it allows time out. In that vein, I've booked a spa day for me and Craig. Result. Plus a healthy deposit into our relationship piggy bank.

Chapter 6
Sharing is caring

29 April 2015

After filling in their mammoth form, I'm now waiting for the clinic to contact me about arranging a date to go in for my blood test. Now that I've more or less decided I want to go for it, I'm very eager to get moving and to find out if I'm eligible. I was hoping we might be able to go at the weekend, and I was dangerously close to the boundary of pleasantly neurotic/full-blown crazy person, checking my emails every half an hour. In the end, I gave up and called them (needy, I know). They said the doctor would be looking at my form soon and would be in touch. That would sound perfectly reasonable to any person in a healthy state of mind. I fear I may not be that person.

My mum came round for a cup of tea and a cuddle and we had a long chat about egg sharing and looked at all the options, reading through the many leaflets I keep in my new 'TTC folder' in detail.

I'm calmer now and better on the whole. I'm always in a rush and want answers instantly, but I need to calm the hell down. It doesn't matter if it's a few more weeks before I know if I'm eligible. If anything, the delay gives me time to ponder it all properly and to decide if I'm a hundred percent OK with it. Plus, we still have options if I'm not eligible – so stay CALM!

4 May 2015
Month 23

I'm feeling OK. My period started yesterday, but I knew it would. We were all away for the weekend for my mum's sixtieth, which was a lot of fun, so I wasn't too upset. Plus we now have the date for the blood test to find out if I'm eligible for egg sharing, and it's this Saturday, so not long to wait. I managed to reign in my neediness and not stare at my phone too much while waiting to hear. A brief interlude – when I lived with Lisa, after uni, she'd send herself loopy waiting for the latest guy to text or call after a date, so I'd make her put her phone in a drawer so she'd stop fiddling with it. That's what I've felt like, as I've been waiting for news. Only the stakes are higher. Instead of wondering whether I'm going to get a second date, it's *am I a step closer to having a baby*? I'm a bit jittery, but I do feel positive – excited, even – like there might be some light at the end of the very long tunnel. It feels good that (hopefully) someone is going to help. I discussed egg sharing with Cait and she thought it was a good idea too. All in all, things are OK at the moment.

9 May 2015

Today we made our first trip to Manchester Fertility for the blood and urine test. After a stressful start due to the motorway being closed (Google maps didn't think to mention that when I checked the route the night before – humph) and us rocking up late, all went smoothly. The clinic has a very different feel to the NHS hospital. They were expecting us, for a start, and knew why we there. No one shouted 'infertility' at me, or asked if I'm pregnant. It felt calm, friendly and welcoming. Also, they have free tea and biscuits!

The urine test was fine, as I thought it would be, although I had been holding my breath every time I passed someone smoking, to be on the safe side. I said this jokingly to the nurse and she told me a tale about woman who had failed the test because she'd been in a bar where they were smoking shishas. Eek. Once that happens, you can't egg share. No retest allowed.

I have to wait a week for the blood test result, so I might have to put my phone in a drawer for at least some of the time. Fingers crossed for an AMH of more than twelve, but let's not obsess too much.

I was OK with the blood test. I was a bit concerned after acupuncture-gate, but all fine. Perhaps the difference is they weren't claiming it'd be nice and relaxing for me. I sat up on the bed and chatted to the nice woman as she did it and I didn't go dizzy or anything, not even a little bit. That's progress.

13 May 2015

I'm in the bath after work when my phone rings. Luckily it's on top of the toilet, not in a drawer. I dry my hands and reach for it. 'Manchester Fertility' shows on the screen. My heart leaps into my mouth. This is it.

'Hello, this is Andrea from Manchester Fertility.'

'Hi!' I trill, then try to lower my voice a few octaves. 'Hello.'

'I'm calling with the results of your blood test.'

'Yes?'

'Your AMH is twenty-seven.'

'Twenty-seven?' I sit up straight in the bath, water sloshing over the edge.

'Yes, it's good news.'

'So I'm eligible to egg share?'

'Yes, you are.'

Amazing! I only needed twelve, it's like I've got an A* when I needed a C to get through. I'm delighted. Finally some good news. I have a good ovarian reserve after all, better than average for my age in fact, so I should respond well to treatment. Yippee! It does make me wonder why I haven't got pregnant so far. I guess it really is just One of Those Things.

The cost is peanuts compared to what we were considering handing over, and less than half what it would have cost us to go to the Czech Republic. This way we don't have to use up lots of leave, or leave Emma behind again. I'm still – I mean *we're* still – going to take time off for the treatment, but it'll be during summer holidays, so we can spend time with Emma too.

The next step is to go to the clinic for a full day. We both have tests so they can see for themselves what they're dealing with. Me a scan, and Craig a semen analysis. We both see the doctor and a counsellor. Finally, it's all happening. We go to Turkey next week, so the timing of the appointment is perfect.

I'm not sure now whether to tell people 1) that we're having IVF 2) that I'm sharing my eggs. In theory, I'd like to keep it all quiet, so I don't have to keep lots of people updated on every step, but it's not in my nature to keep things to myself, and when people ask, I want to tell them. Hmm. If it was down to Craig, no one would know anything. He's an introvert – in the true sense of the word. I don't mean he's shy or socially awkward – he's not at all – but he likes to work things through in his own mind, whereas I like to share with others and discuss.

We did consider not telling Emma, in case it upset her in some way. I'm never quite sure what she'll be sensitive about. But now I've told a few friends, we have to tell Emma in case it comes out at some point. Hopefully she'll take it in her stride and not be worried about it. I'll pick my timing and wording carefully. Conversations with teenagers can be like tiptoeing through a landmine and trying to reach the other side safely, but sometimes getting halfway, admitting defeat and retreating, feeling dissatisfied and irked. Other times Emma surprises me with her maturity and emotional intelligence. I hope it's the latter for this particular conversation.

Craig got annoyed with me earlier. He was in the room when I was on the phone to

Lisa, giving her the latest on the fertility exhibition.

'So, there are deals where you can get money back if it doesn't work, or there's another option which might be a bit controversial...' I'm saying, when Craig looks up from what he's doing with and fixes me with a stare. I shrivel and falter. 'What?' I ask defensively and leave the room so I don't feel self-conscious. I feel like I've been caught being naughty.

'I thought we weren't telling people,' he says to me afterwards.

'No, we didn't agree that. We said we'd *consider* whether to tell people and I did consider it.'

'Well, it's up to you.'

'So, why are you being so funny about it then?' My stomach is churning. I hate this sort of confrontation. He doesn't usually say anything about stuff like this, so if he's making a point he must feel strongly about it.

'I'm not being *funny*. This isn't the latest gossip to chat about with your mates. You're married now and you have a family. What you do doesn't only affect you.' Ouch that stings. 'We said we might not tell Emma. We'll have to if you're running round telling people. Imagine if she heard about it from someone else.'

'We'll tell her then.' I'm sullen, hanging my head, embarrassed and upset.

'What did Lisa say?'

'She said it was a lovely idea, and that

she'd do it in my situation.'

He nods.

'See? No big drama. She was fine with it.'

'Well, what if she wasn't? People can have strong views on the subject and I'm concerned that'd change how you feel about it.'

'I'd like to think I know my own mind better than that,' I scoff, but deep down I know he might have a point.

I'm now confused about who to tell what. I guess it's a sensitive topic and it's not surprising emotions are running high. I did feel very mixed up about our conversation, but it made me realise how well we've been doing so far. It would have been easy to get into lots of arguments.

20 May 2015

I told Emma about the egg sharing. Happily, she was fine about it. Her initial response was, 'So do they take the nucleus out of the cell before your egg is shared?' Erm, not the response I was expecting at all. It's a long time since my GCSE Biology, but I'm fairly confident I remember that a nucleus is pretty essential to a cell's structure. What she was driving at was, if the IVF worked for the recipient of my donation, would the baby born have my DNA and be biologically mine? The answer is obviously yes. This took a bit of consideration on her part, but we had an open and honest conversation about it all, and she agreed that it was a good thing to do. She did say she wouldn't be comfortable with Craig donating his sperm, but as Emma and I are not biologically related, she wouldn't be biologically related to any babies born from my egg, so in her mind that's all OK. Phew. It's a relief to have it out in the open. Now I'm free to tell people if and when it comes up, if I want to.

Although I did have a strange thought that the more people who know, the more chance there is that someone I tell could know the recipient and make the connection. I know it's unlikely, but I guess it's about feeling in control. Perhaps this is something to discuss with the counsellor. See, I do like discussing.

It was our second wedding anniversary on Monday, so we went away for the weekend. We stayed at a quirky little place called the Vintage Showman's Caravan, which had an outdoor bath heated by a wood burner. We went for a walk and found a nice cosy pub for a pint of cider.

'I guess we won't be able to do this as easily when we have a baby,' I say.

'You're right, we should make the most of it.' Craig smiles. I smile back, but it's a weak attempt. I feel empty inside. It's our second anniversary. We've been trying for a baby for two years. I didn't see myself here on our wedding day, or even on our first anniversary. I was sure I'd at *least* be pregnant by this point.

I study the menu. 'We could come back here for dinner later,' I say. 'The food looks good.' I'm trying. I feel annoyed with myself. I love weekends away, just the two of us, but it feels like we're treading water, and I'm waiting, waiting, waiting. Waiting for test results, waiting for appointments, waiting for the next bit of news. I should stop – there is only the present moment and I'm wasting it by worrying about the future.

30 May 2015
Month 24

Month 24. Wow. So it's the twenty-fourth month of trying to conceive. Two years, which means we're officially described as infertile by the medical profession. Nice. As suspected, the diagnosis is unexplained infertility in our case.

2 June 2015

Tomorrow we go to the clinic for our full day of stuff. In preparation, I've had to write a sort of dating ad for the potential recipient of my eggs. Weird. I also had to write a note to any potential child who might be born from my egg. Even more weird. Here's what I wrote to the potential recipient:

> *So this is odd – feels a bit like writing a dating ad for my eggs. What can I say about me? You'll probably want to know upfront – I'm reasonable looking, I mean I wouldn't*

say I'm a super model, but I'm definitely a long way from Quasimodo.

I like to keep in shape. I love running and have done a lot of races in the past. Chasing a new personal best used to be my thing, but I now run purely for enjoyment, for the thinking time and to get some endorphins pumping. In a past life I was a fitness instructor, so physical fitness has always been important to me.

My profession is Marketing and Communications. I went to uni and have a degree in Communications. I've since done professional qualifications in Marketing and Internal Communication. I enjoy my job and am moderately ambitious – not quite Alan Sugar style, but bags more oomph than, say, Wayne and Waynetta slob.

In terms of hobbies, I love reading (anything I can get my hands on). I love cooking (and eating), travelling to new places and seeing different cultures. Long walks in the country and…oh no, sorry, it's all gone a bit too 'dating ad'. Back to characteristics you might like to see in your future child…

I'd describe myself as calm and level-headed. I tend to think things

*through before reacting, and others
may describe me as on the quieter
end of the scale. I'm definitely not
loud or shouty, but I have lots of
friends, like to chat and can spend
hours on the phone to my mum or
best friend.*

*I live with my husband and step-
daughter. We're a happy family and
all have our fingers crossed for a new
addition in the not too distant future.*

Pretty heavy stuff, isn't it? I was aiming
to get across that I'm reasonably intelligent,
have a sense of humour and am fit and healthy,
without wanting to blow my own trumpet. I am
British after all. Hope she wants me/my eggs.

4 June 2015

So much to update on. I'd like to be able
to download my thoughts onto the paper
without having to write it all out. So tired after a
full day at the clinic – set off at 7 a.m. and got
home at 8.30 p.m.

- Our day involved:
- Dildo cam scan (me)
- Semen analysis (C)
- Counsellor (both)
- Chat with egg donor lady (both)
- Wee test (me)
- Chat with nurse (both)
- Blood tests (both)

- Long chat with doctor (both)

I felt absolutely drained by the end of it all, but it was worthwhile and things are moving along nicely. The scan was to look at the follicles in my ovaries, which gives an indication of how well I might respond to the treatment. They look for a minimum of four to five follicles and I had eleven, so again, I got an A* there.

Craig did similarly well in his semen analysis. Anything over 25 million sperm is classed as normal and he had 68 million. On paper we're both in top notch condition – hence our 'unexplained infertility' diagnoses. All of these things look hopeful for IVF working, and the doc estimated a forty percent chance of success. I'm excited, it's finally happening.

The blood test was horrible. They're testing for loads of things, but since my brain turned to mush during our intensive day, the only ones I can remember are HIV and if I'm a cystic fibrosis carrier. If I am, I can't egg share, but it would only be an issue for us as a couple if Craig was too. Because they're testing for so many things, they needed six vials of blood. I was sitting down, but in a chair with an upright back. I'd got cocky and didn't mention my aversion to needles, as I've been OK with it. It took ages and I could feel the needle moving in my arm as the nurse unscrewed one vial and attached the next one. Blugh.

'Are you OK?' the nurse asks I've obviously turned my fetching shade of green.

'Yes, I will be, just carry on,' I say, feeling cold sweat prickling the back of my neck.

'OK, I know how you feel. I'm scared of flying. We're near the airport here and I don't even like seeing the planes fly over. They think I'm mad here, but I can't even look. I turn away and hide my eyes.'

I try to smile, thinking *hurry up! Please hurry up!* She unscrews a vial and I feel the needle twist slightly in my vein. I close my eyes and try to breathe slowly and deeply and put my mind somewhere else. She's pressing some cotton wool into the crook of my elbow.

'Is it done?' I ask, eyes still shut.

'I've got five vials, so we still need one more, but you looked like you needed a break.' *Nooooo* – that means I have to start again.

'When you're ready, go sit in the waiting room and have a biscuit. We'll come back for you when you're feeling better.'

Great.

'Are you OK?' Craig asks, as the nurse sees me out to reception.

'No, I went green and they haven't finished, so I have to go back in for more blood taking.' He gives me a sympathetic smile and goes off to fetch me some sugary tea and a biscuit. Luckily, the final one is fine, as it's quick. I now know I'm OK with short ones, but if they want a lot of blood, I'm not. My arm is sore now, too.

Next, we meet with the counsellor. A warm and calm lady, not much older than me.

She has a neat blonde bob. She sits with her legs crossed to one side, the toe of her beige court shoe tapping the leg of the chair.

'So, you're thinking of becoming a very special person,' she opens.

'Sorry?'

'You're thinking of donating your eggs.'

'Oh, well, yes.'

She smiles warmly. 'It's a wonderful thing to do, giving hope to another couple and possibly creating a new family.'

I beam at her.

'But it's important to think through all the implications and be sure you're happy with it. It's a big decision and there's no going back from it. The laws changed recently so that any child born from a donor egg can contact the Human Fertilisation and Embryo Authority when they turn eighteen and find out their donor's name. The HFEA can put the child and donor in touch.' She pauses, waiting for a reaction.

'Oh, so they wouldn't just turn up on my doorstep unannounced?'

'No. That would make a better film plot, but no.' She smiles. 'It's usually just curiosity on the child's part, to see where they came from. They already have a family and they're not looking for a mum. Generally one meeting is all it takes to satisfy their curiosity and they carry on with their lives.'

'Yes, I've thought about that and decided there are worse things that could happen than someone born from my donated egg wanting to meet me.'

She nods steepling her fingers in front of her chest. 'Now, we do encourage openness and honesty between parents and their children, both for women who've donated eggs and women who've received donated eggs. We have some books to help young children understand.' She gestured towards a bookshelf. 'They explain all the facts in an age-appropriate way, so that there are no surprises later in life which could lead to confusion about identity, or resentment.'

'That makes sense,' I said, eyeing the picture books she was referring to.

'The other reason we encourage openness is that there's a remote possibility that your child could meet a child born from your egg, not know they were biologically half-siblings and start a sexual relationship.' Woah - what? I hadn't thought of that!

'Wow, yes I guess that makes sense.'

'It's a very slim chance, but you never know.'

She asked us questions about our relationship, how Craig felt about me donating eggs, how we'd feel if it worked for the other couple but not us, whether I would want to find out if it had worked for the other couple (no, well not straight away, anyway. Possibly at some point in the future, just so I'd know if my future child has a half-sibling). It was all very thought-provoking and I still feel good about the decision, just completely drained.

So the next steps are, we wait (yes, more waiting) for the test results, which could take up to an agonising five weeks. Assuming all is OK, they then show my profile (dating ad) to a woman they will match me to based on our physical characteristics. She'll have been waiting for a donor for a while, so hopefully she'll decide quickly and say yes. Then they have to synch her periods to mine, so we're at the same point in our cycles at the same time. They do this by putting her on the pill. This takes four to six weeks, depending on how un-synched we are to start off with. *Then* when I get my period, I inject myself in the stomach every day for two weeks. The injections are to stimulate my ovaries to prepare and release lots of eggs at the same time, instead of the usual one egg. They check my hormone levels a few times during the two weeks with (more) blood tests. Then when my hormone levels show my eggs are ripe for the plucking, they sedate me and whip them out. Apparently it's painful if you're awake. They pop them in a petri dish with Craig's sperm, and then we wait (my favourite thing). We wait to see if any have fertilised, then we wait to see if any fertilised eggs – now embryos – make it to day five. If they do, they put one back in me (yay!) then we *wait* TWO WEEKS then do a pregnancy test at home. Phew.

I'm crossing everything that all this will happen by August, which is about do-able, though it would be tight with all the things that need to happen. The clinic seems to think it'd be possible.

My eyes want to close now and my

hand is cramping from writing. I need to go to sleep. Night night.

8 June 2015

Feeling much better after getting a few good nights' sleep in a row. Guess that's something to be thankful for and hopefully something I won't be able to take for granted soon ☺ It got me thinking, and when I've looked back through my writing, I can see there's a direct correlation between the times I've felt low and being tired. Something as simple as being well rested definitely makes me feel better – if not happier, at least more equipped to deal with whatever situation I'm presented with.

Tip #9 Get enough sleep

Seriously, get enough sleep. It sounds like basic stuff, but the power of a good night's sleep is not to be underestimated. Scientists tell us sleep is essential to our physical and mental health and the effects of not getting enough good quality sleep can manifest themselves in pretty scary ways. According to the NHS website, the cost of lots of sleepless nights is not only irritability and a lack of focus, but regular poor sleep puts you at risk of serious medical conditions, including obesity, heart disease, depression and anxiety. Yikes!

23 June 2015

'If you die part way through the treatment, do you give your permission for me to continue?' We're sitting at the kitchen table, filling out a hundred-and-one forms for the clinic. Egg sharing sure is admin-heavy.

'Yes.'

'So I'd have your baby after you're dead? That's so sad!'

'Well, you wouldn't have to.'

'So I'd lose you and a potential baby?'

'I'm not planning on going anywhere.'

'No, OK, let's just tick yes then,' I say. 'Next question: If I die, or become mentally incapacitated do I give my permission for them to continue with the treatment for the other couple? Wow, this is pretty heavy going stuff, isn't it? Yes, it has to be yes, doesn't it?'

Craig shrugs, then nods.

I tick 'Yes'. 'How many couples am I willing to donate my eggs to?' I say. 'What do they mean? I'm only donating to one couple, the woman I'm matched to.'

Craig peers over my shoulder. 'Maybe it's a standard form they use for all egg donors, not just egg sharers.'

'Hmm, that'd make sense. Shall I put one, then?' I answer my own question. 'I might just leave it blank and ask when we hand them in.' I'm starting to feel a bit out of my depth. It's all so *serious*. Am I just having a bit of a wobble or is there more to it? I think it's the form flummoxing me and making me feel out of control. Hopefully once I get my questions answered I'll feel better.

The other thing that's playing on my mind is still the whole telling people/not telling people issue. Craig has told no one at all. He snapped a question at me during the *doo-doo-doo* of a Skype call to his brother and Mickey, asking me if we were going to tell them. Talk about a panic response. I said no. We've spoken about it since, though, and he said it's because he hasn't thought through whether he wants to tell people, and he's concerned that people might react negatively. If that's the case, then it's fine. The reason I've felt a bit anxious about Craig's not wanting to tell people is that I've been worried he's not completely comfortable with what we're doing. He says he is comfortable with me donating my eggs as long as I am, so now I need to make sure I am.

It's weird because I've felt completely fine with it for the last two months and now suddenly I'm all of a dither. The thought that's niggling me is I probably wouldn't have considered egg sharing initially if it wasn't so much cheaper, and I don't want the decision to be about saving money. I'm going to try to work out what my fears are and whether they're justified.

Fear #1
Not understanding exactly what is going to happen to my donated eggs.
Justified?
Yes, but I can sort this by speaking to the clinic.

Fear #2

Anxiety caused by telling/not telling people and how Craig feels about it.
Justified?
Not really, we can sort this by discussing and deciding.

Fear #3
How would I feel if IVF didn't work for us? I wouldn't necessarily have to find out if it worked for the other couple, but would I be wondering? Would it matter?
Justified?
Yes. Need to give this some more consideration.

Fear #4
That I wouldn't like or approve of the couple who get my eggs.
Justified?
No. This shouldn't be a factor. I'm donating to a couple who must really want a baby, so I trust that that's enough.

Fear #5
That I'd feel odd about it afterwards.
Justified?
No. Don't think I'd care once I had a baby.

Fear #6
That it somehow lessens my chances of it working.
Justified?
No, it shouldn't do and we can always try again, anyway.

Fear #7
Other people's reactions.
Justified?
No, doesn't matter.

Fear #8
That I'm not a hundred percent comfortable with my eggs being taken away, mixed with a stranger's sperm, then put into another woman's body.
Justified?
Am I? This is the biggie.

I have the opportunity to help someone else without it causing me too much bother, as I'm having IVF anyway. Altruistic donors donate when they're not having treatment themselves. They have the hormone injections, endure being closely monitored and having their eggs collected, all for the benefit of someone else. That's quite an ask and I take my hat off to them.

I want my motive for doing it to be because I feel good about being able to help someone else and because it feels 'right'. Not because it saves money or because I'd feel guilty about changing my mind. I read an article in the *Guardian* about egg donation and I feel reassured. All my fears are normal and a healthy part of the decision-making process. This quote from 'Sarah' who had a baby through donor eggs says it all: 'We were given our donor's hair colour, eye colour and blood group. All I could think about was the fact that her hair colour was a bit lighter than mine. When you only have a few things to go on, they become momentous. I spoke to my mum for reassurance and when I put down the phone, I suddenly thought – the donor is someone who doesn't know me and is prepared to go through all of this to help a complete stranger. If I want my child to inherit a characteristic, would it be my hair colour or would it be being that selfless and wonderful a person?'

It made me feel all choked up, and I realised what it all boils down to is I have the chance to do something amazing for someone else. OK, so not quite as amazing as an altruistic donor, but I can be a little bit amazing. I'm going to do it.

30 June 2015
Month 25

I'm still feeling good about egg sharing. It was good to ask myself the questions and to make sure I'm comfortable, and I am. Craig told his mum and dad on Saturday and they were fine about it. They both said it sounded like a nice thing to do and he was relieved. I'm glad it's out there so it's not 'taboo'.

So, my problem now is I'm waiting again. My period has come a bit early, which means my next one is due 29/30 July. In order to go ahead in August, I'll need to start injections at that point. I still have to get my test results, get matched and get synched. I'm very tense that it won't happen in time. I've emailed egg-sharing lady at the clinic, but got her 'Out of Office' until tomorrow.

I'm not that busy at work and all I'm doing is dwelling on it, overthinking, waiting and worrying. I'm getting on my own nerves. I should know better, but I'm wallowing and pandering to myself. It's hard to stop, but I know I should. OK, I'll try now. Properly I mean.

1 July 2015

Had the news I've been waiting for! Blood test results are back and everything is fine. Yay! My dating ad has been sent to a potential match - eek! She could be looking at it right now and deciding. Big day for her, too. I hope she's excited and likes the sound of me. Apparently she's said she wanted someone tall and sporty. I'm not sure I'd describe myself as 'sporty', but I am into fitness and I did include working in a gym and running in my ad, so I guess that's why egg-sharing lady thought of me. She gets a little while to decide, but the good thing is, she's already on the pill in preparation (my kind of woman) so there's no need for synching. She'll stop taking it the week before my period is due and voilà, we're synched. Magic.

I have an appointment to go to the clinic to be shown how to do the injections, then, all being well, I'll be able to start them when my next period starts. So excited! They asked me to download an app and watch a video of how to do them. It looks straightforward enough and not too scary. I've watched it several times. Hopefully I won't go green and/or faint every day. It's really happening now. It all feels so close. Please let it all go to plan – and work!

5 July 2015

More news – my potential match has said, 'Yes'! She's now my official match. It only took her a day to decide, and apparently she'd turned down two others (cheeky) so I must be a catch. Ha ha. Can't help feel a bit flattered. So, we're full steam ahead now. All I'm waiting for is my appointment to be shown how to do the injections, and then for my period to arrive and it all begins. Odd to be looking forward to my period for once.

After so long, there finally *is* light at the end of the tunnel. We might finally get to where we want to be. I have to keep in mind that I know I'll be able to cope if it doesn't work. I won't be any worse off than I am now, so I'm going to be excited, not scared or worried. I have nothing to lose, but everything to gain – wasn't that a Kylie Minogue song in the eighties? Anyway, I've booked the middle two weeks of August off work, and by the start of September we'll know if it's worked. I could be pregnant in less than two months. Oh my.

19 July 2015

I bought a hypnotherapy package from

the Fertile Mind. I listen to a relaxation track each night before I go to sleep. It includes calming music and uses visualisation and breathing techniques. This phase is all about preparing myself. The track I'm listening to now asks me to visualise what a healthy environment inside my body would look like, when everything is working as it should. I visualise a luscious green garden for some reason, and I see lots of plants growing and flowers blossoming.

Once I start the treatment, there are different tracks to listen to and there will be different ones again after the embryo is put in. Russell calls the two week wait – that is, the wait from having the embryo put in to doing the pregnancy test – the 'two week thrive', as it's the time for you and your embryo to thrive. There's also a passage to read each day to help you stay calm and relaxed, and an activity sheet to fill out. It's making me feel supported and in control and calm, so that's a win already.

Chapter 7
Needles galore

22 July 2015

On the train to London again and feeling invigorated. We went to the clinic on Monday and collected our medication. Our fridge looks like a pharmacy! Part of the medication needs to be kept in the fridge, then there's another massive bag which I've stored under the bed out of the way. I had a practise injecting myself with a blank needle and it wasn't actually that bad. The needle is only an inch long and very thin. You have to pinch a bit of skin near your belly button, then push it in. It doesn't hurt and it didn't bleed or anything afterwards. Quite surprising that you can stab yourself without any ill effects. It took me a few minutes to pluck up the courage – it went against all my natural instincts, but with Craig next to me and the nurse watching expectantly, social decorum dictated I get on with it, and overruled my fear.

I do the first injection on the first full day of my period. So if my period starts in the afternoon, I start my injections the next day. I start injecting myself with one type of hormone to encourage my follicles to ripen a load of eggs, then after five days I start a second lot of injections at the same time. This stops the eggs being released and setting off down my fallopian tubes (that'd be no good, as they need to be carefully collected at the right time). Once they're nicely ripe, I do a 'trigger' shot at a very specific time. It has to be exactly thirty-six hours before my eggs are to be collected. The nerve-wracking thing is, there are so many points at which it could go wrong. First of all, I might not respond well to the treatment and they might not be able to collect any eggs. Assuming that bit goes OK, my eggs might not become fertilised when they put them with Craig's sperm. Then assuming they do become fertilised – or at least some of them do – they have to continue to develop and to turn into 'blastocysts' after five days. If this doesn't happen, there'll be no embryo to put back in.

So the month will look like this:

Day 1 – period starts
Day 2 – injection
Day 3 – injection
Day 4 – injection
Day 5 – blood test, injection
Day 6 – injection x 2
Day 7 – injection x2
Day 8 – blood test, scan, injection x 2
Day 9 – injection x2
Day 10 – blood test, scan, injection x 2
Day 11 – injection x2
Day 12 – injection x2, TRIGGER SHOT
Day 13 – nothing
Day 14 – egg collection, we find out how many eggs they collected (hopefully ten to twenty)
Day 15 – we eagerly await a phone call to let us know how many were fertilised
Day 16 – wait
Day 17 – update on how many are still

developing
Day 18 – the transfer. An embryo is put in (fingers crossed)
Day 19-29 – I insert pessaries every morning and night
Day 30 – pregnancy test

An exciting, but terrifying, month ahead. I hope I'll be well and truly over any fear of needles by the end of it. I will do my best to stay calm and positive. The hypnotherapy is helping with that. I like listening to it before I go to sleep and visualising my healthy colour. I imagine my eggs as seeds and my embryo as a seed with a tiny sprout, and my womb the garden where it will be planted and grow. It might sound a bit weird, but hey.

Once the embryo is transferred, the hypnotherapy programme is all about welcoming it and creating the best environment for the pregnancy to thrive by harnessing your unconscious mind. It does make a lot of sense, but I guess even if my hypnotherapy doesn't actually affect the outcome, it makes me feel as though I'm doing all I can to give IVF the best chance. And it's better than acupuncture!

1 August 2015
Month 26

IVF month! My period started yesterday, so I'm all geared up to do my first injection tonight. Important things to remember, courtesy of Russell:

Stay calm and relaxed, so my body is ready to welcome the embryo.

Stay in the present. Nothing can predict the future, not even my thinking.

Whatever happens, I'll be OK.

Wish me luck!

2 August 2015
Day 1 of IVF

The first stab is done. As it grew closer to 7 p.m. (stab time), I began to feel more and more nervous. The medication is in the fridge and I decided it made sense to do the injection at the kitchen table after dinner, so Emma and Craig were both there. I washed my hands and cleaned an area of my tummy with the sterile wipe and dialled up the correct dosage on the pen.

'What if I do it wrong?' I look at Craig anxiously.

'You won't. You've watched the videos and read the leaflets, you know what to do.'

'It'll be fine, Mum. Just do it.' Emma is standing next to me. Well, I'm going to have to do it. Before I lose my nerve, I pinch an inch, as they'd shown me in the clinic, and push the needle in. It slides in easily with just a slight sting and I allow myself to breathe. But then I'm stuck.

'I can't reach the plunger,' I say to Craig, panicked. The needle is like a big pen with a button on the end to push the liquid out, and the way I'm holding it means my thumb isn't at the right angle to push the button.

'Take it out and start again.'

'I can't. I don't want to do it again. You do it.'

And so I hold it in place while Craig presses the button.

'Slowly!'

'I am doing it slowly. There, all done.'

Phew. I pull the needle out and it sort of twangs my skin on the last bit. Blurgh. I feel myself going a bit dizzy, but a few deep breaths and I'm right as rain. I'm sure tomorrow will be fine, now I know what to expect. All in all it's a success. I'm not moody or emotional yet – just excited.

5 August 2015
Day 4

Oh, this is hard. The second stab went fine, except I forgot to hold the needle in for ten seconds after the plunger was all the way down before taking it out – they tell you to do this, not sure why. I don't think it's a big deal as all the liquid went in, but I was determined to do it perfectly on day 3. Then last night was a disaster! The same thing as the first night happened. I was holding the pen thing awkwardly.

'I'm stuck again. I need you to push it in for me.'

'You can do it, just move your hand a

bit,' Craig says, a bit impatiently.

'I can't move my hand, I'll make the needle wiggle. Please help me.' I'm aware this is making me sound like a wet lettuce. I'm usually a reasonably confident and level-headed grown-up, but IVF has regressed me to a self-doubting, timid adolescent.

He sighs and takes hold of the pen and starts pushing the button in, while I hold the pen steady. After a few seconds, I feel wet on my tummy.

'Stop!' I say. 'It's leaked.'

'Shit!'

'We've wasted some, what do we do? I won't have had the right dose.' I feel the panic rising and curse myself for letting it happen.

'OK, well just put some more in.'

'But how much?? If I use more, we'll run out before the end. I'm going to ring the clinic.'

Thankfully they were understanding and didn't make me feel any more stupid than I already felt. They advised dialling up another 100ul from a fresh pen. It looked like there was enough left in the current pen, so I used that, but then there wasn't and I got myself in such a tizz that I ended up doing four separate injections all in all, and I couldn't be sure whether I'd had the right dosage.

'It's done now. You've corrected it and you'll do it right tomorrow.' Craig is using his stern voice, which is how he'd tell himself off, but not what I need at all.

'I'm already feeling distressed that I've messed the whole thing up and you're not helping by speaking to me like that,' I say, trying hard not to cry. I run off upstairs so we can both cool off. He's seriously irritating me. I know I shouldn't be stressed, which is making me more and more stressed and upset in a perpetual cycle.

He was nice to me when he came up to bed, but I couldn't sleep. I laid awake trying to work out if I'd had the right dosage and what it might mean if I hadn't. I eventually fell into a fitful sleep, dreaming about needles squirting out liquid onto the floor and me trying to scoop it up before it soaked in. Needless to say, I was not calm.

I felt better today and I did my injection perfectly tonight – fourth time's the charm. From tomorrow I'll have to start doing the second injection, too. That one involves mixing powder with liquid, then using a syringe to suck liquid out of a vial and making sure it has no air bubbles in it. Yikes. It's quite a lot of pressure to get right on your own.

All today I've felt quite emotional and odd. I've had some period-like cramps, but a bit different. Sort of like my womb is tight and heavy. It all feels very surreal, like it's not really happening. It's very strange.

I go to the clinic for my blood test in the morning. My mum is coming with me as Craig can't get the time off work. I hope everything is progressing as it should. We have to set off at

6.15 a.m. to get there on time, because traffic to Manchester is a nightmare in the morning. Right, going to have a bath and try to RELAX!

6 August 2015
Day 5

Feeling loads better today. Had my blood test and everything is progressing as it should. We're on track to start the second lot of injections tonight. I told the nurse about my mishap and she was sympathetic and not too concerned. Phew.

I go in again on Monday for another blood test and a scan to see how my eggs are doing, then I'm likely to be ready for egg collection end of next week. I'm off work for two weeks after tomorrow, which will be good. I've been working from home today after my appointment, which has been lovely. It's nice not to have too much pressure, just enough so it's a distraction.

My womb area feels full and achy. I kind of like it, as it's telling me my body is doing something different. I've had absolutely loads of egg white! Guess that makes sense as I'll be super fertile. We're not allowed to have sex at all during this period, as in theory ten or twenty eggs could get fertilised, which would leave me in a bit of a pickle.

So, tonight's challenge is to mix the powder stuff and load up the syringe. I've watched some YouTube videos, so I'm feeling fairly positive about it. I'll stay calm and focused and it'll go smoothly.

9 August 2015
Day 8

Just got back from a weekend in Cheltenham for a friend's fortieth birthday party. It was good fun. We all went and I'm glad we did. I was concerned about having to transport the medication, but I took it in a cool bag and popped it in the fridge when I got there. I did the stab in my friend's bedroom and she came with me, which was good as she's been through IVF herself several times (none of them successful, sadly). She had some handy hints and tips for getting all the liquid out of the vial and for getting rid of air bubbles without squirting the liquid out.

I've done my two stabs tonight all by myself and all went fine. The first one is easy peasy now, the second one fricking hurts! I have to push quite hard before it actually punctures the skin, then it stings afterwards and I get a red itchy patch where it went in. It's like the first one was a gateway injection and now I'm doing the hardcore one.

I'm feeling calmer generally. It's so easy to panic over every minor thing, but I have to learn to let it go and trust that everything will be OK. Or if it's not, that I'll be OK.

It's another blood test and scan tomorrow. They'll tell me how many follicles I have, which should give an idea of how many eggs they're likely to collect. Exciting! It'll be another early start. I'm shattered from driving back from Cheltenham, so it'll be an early night tonight.

All in all, still feeling OK physically, too. The only side effects I'm aware of are my mouth tasting like a hospital and the full, aching feeling, low down in my tummy. I can cope with both of those.

12 August 2015
Day 11

I've been to the clinic twice since I last wrote. I had a scan and a blood test on Monday morning and the same again this morning. All is looking good, I have lots of follicles developing. I saw them on the screen. They wouldn't tell me how many as it 'raises expectations', but they said not to worry, as it looks like I'll get plenty of eggs. So I won't worry. I don't feel worried, I feel relaxed, happy and excited!

So I do my last two stabs tonight, then have to set the alarm for 1 a.m. to get up and do the trigger shot. I go in on Friday to have my eggs collected. Woo!

14 August 2015
Day 13

My eggs have been collected! There were fifteen – yay! That's eight for me and seven for egg recipient lady. I'm pleased with that. The doctor said it's a good number, because if it's a lot higher, the quality can be compromised.

The collection wasn't too bad at all. I didn't know anything about it. It was a deep sedation, which is one step away from a general anaesthetic. It's weird, I remember being in the room looking at the lights on the ceiling and then nothing until they woke me up. It's like being switched off. The anaesthetist put the needle in the back of my hand and said, 'Here's your gin and tonic' (what a card), then asked me to count back from ten. I got to eight, then the lights on the ceiling started to go fuzzy, then I just went.

When I came round I was giggling, and when they asked me if I was OK, all I could say was, 'I'm really drunk'. That's how I felt. Maybe he wasn't kidding about the gin and tonic. I couldn't take anything in for a good twenty minutes until I'd 'sobered up'.

I'm pretty much feeling OK now, just a slight achiness and I'm bleeding a bit, but that's normal. It's a similar feeling to when I had dye put in my tubes. Guess it's being messed about with in a similar way. I have to take some antibiotics so I don't get an infection and I have to start using the pessaries/suppositories. I get a choice – front or back. Lucky me! This will keep my womb lining at the right thickness for an embryo to implant. No more needles at least!

Tonight, my eight eggs are with Craig's sixty-eight million sperm getting romantic. They'll call us in the morning to say how many have been fertilised. The doc said to expect around seventy percent, so that's around five or six. Then, all being well, I'll go back on Wednesday to have an embryo put in.

15 August 2015
Day 14

My phone didn't leave my side from the moment I woke up up to when it finally rang (no time for putting it in the drawer at this stage). I stared at it as I munched my way through cereal which tasted like cardboard. I balanced it on top of the bathroom cabinet while I had a shower, turning the water off every two minutes, just in case the sound of it drowned out the sound of ringing. I laid it on the bed where I could keep a close eye on it while I got dressed. I carried it downstairs and placed it carefully on the arm of the settee as I flicked mindlessly through TV channels. As I was pacing the kitchen, holding onto the phone, it rang, causing me to jump out of my skin. I quickly turned the kettle off. I couldn't have any background noise interfering.

'Hello, is that Tori Day?'
'Yes.'
'Three eggs have fertilised.'
Three? Out of eight? That sounds low.
'OK.'
'So we'll provisionally book you an appointment for a transfer the day after tomorrow, then we'll call you that morning to let you know whether to come in, or whether we'll wait for a five day blastocyst transfer.'

Or whether I get to come in for any sort of transfer at all, I can't help silently adding. I thank the embryologist and hang up, feeling deflated.

Craig is in the bedroom doing yoga. He sees me coming, clutching at my phone, and immediately comes out of his downward dog.

'Have they called?'

'Yes. Three eggs fertilised.'

'Oh, well that's good news.'

'Is it? Three? What was wrong with the other five? I don't think my eggs and your sperm like each other very much.'

'OK, so it could have been higher, but this is further than we've ever got. We have three embryos and we only need one.'

I nod. I need to stay positive.

Unfortunately, I'm having the nagging and rather unhelpful thought that if we didn't share, we'd have more embryos now. I wonder how many of the seven I donated fertilised. Not that it makes any difference to me now. It's going to be a tough couple of days. I might listen to my hypnotherapy thing and see if that makes me feel better. I don't think there's much else to say right now.

16 August 2015
Day 15

I'm feeling a bit better about the three today. I spoke to my IVF friend and she said it'll be the strongest three eggs and sperm. Maybe it will be OK, after all. It's a tense time, but it was always going to be tense, and I think I'm doing a reasonable job of dealing with it.

I'm looking forward to tomorrow's phone call. Just think, I could be pregnant in a couple of days!

17 August 2015
Day 16

'It's good news.'

Oh, thank God, and God bless the embryologist for getting straight to the point.

'Two out of the three embryos are developing nicely and are at the eight cell stage. The other one is at the four cell stage, so still hanging in there, but not looking as strong.'

'OK, so what's next?'

'We recommend waiting to transfer a day 5 blastocyst, so we'll call again in two days to confirm.'

I go upstairs to tell Craig, who has a massive grin on his face at the news.

Then I ring my mum and completely lose it (am a jibbering wreck).

'Hi Mum, it's me.'

'Hi darling, are you OK?'

'Yes.' *break down sobbing*

'What is it? What's happened?' she demands, panic in her voice.

'No, nothing, sorry, it's good news,' I manage to get out between tears. 'We have two really strong embryos and we're going for a day 5 blastocyst transfer.'

'That's great love. Why are you so

upset?'

'I'm not. I don't know. It's just so much.'

'OK love, I know. You're doing so well, and you're nearly there now. Go give Craig a cuddle.'

I completely get why this is described as an emotional rollercoaster. I feel like a lunatic. I'm happy now, but it's a tentative high. Like riding a wave, but knowing you could fall off at any point. This is where living in the moment is important – one day at a time and today is a good day.

18 August 2015
Day 17

Transfer tomorrow, the biggest day so far. They will call in the morning to confirm the embryos are looking good (well, that at least one is looking good), so until that point there's always the fear that something could go wrong, but I'm feeling optimistic. Best case is one to go in and two to freeze, but as long as there's one to go in, I'll be delighted.

I want to write down here, for myself to look back on – I've had some period-like twinges tonight. This is a side effect of the progesterone pessaries. It doesn't mean my period is coming. Very important to remember that over the next two weeks. I'm glad I've felt it now so I can reassure myself later.

19 August 2015
Day 18

The transfer has happened, so I'm now technically pregnant. Bit of a curve ball on the call this morning – neither of the two stronger embryos had quite made it to blastocyst stage. They are 'morulas', which is one step behind. One was looking strong and other not quite as much, so the upshot is – they put both in! They only freeze blastocysts, so if it hadn't gone in, it would have been discarded, so they may as well give it a shot. I could end up with twins, but I'd take two over none! So there we are. We made it to the final step of the procedure and now the testing two week wait (or two week thrive) starts.

I don't know what I was expecting, but the transfer consisted of the embryos being put in what was essentially a long thin floppy straw, which was popped through my cervix (it didn't hurt like the camera). The embryos were then pushed out. I mean, imagine if they'd dropped out of the 'straw' on the way from the lab to my 'lady area'? (Sorry, I can't say vagina, I'm British.) Presumably they've thought it through and the straw is safe, so we'll say no more about it.

So, two embryos are inside me – glued inside me, and it's my job to nurture them so they grow and thrive. I feel calm. It's very exciting, and of course I really hope it works, but I also have in mind that if it doesn't, we'll try again, and I believe one of the times it will. I know what to expect now, and while I wouldn't choose to do it all again, I know I wouldn't be as anxious about the injections. Here's to staying calm and keeping busy!

22 August 2015
Day 21

The embryos have been inside me for four days now and I've had a lot of period-like cramps, particularly during last night and this morning. I'm finding it hard to stay positive as it feels so similar to all the other months when I haven't been pregnant. I'm telling myself I don't know what the feeling is – it could be a side effect of the progesterone pessaries, it could be implantation pain. I don't know what it is, that's the fact. My mind wants to work it out, so it uses past experiences to jump to conclusions about the future. These are just thoughts, not reality. I won't know until I take that test in nine days' time. This is the difficult part. I'm trying to fill my time and keep busy, but I'm bored. I'm glad to be going back to work on Monday, I hope I'll be busy.

We've been off work for two weeks now and not done that much other than go back and forth to the clinic, so we're all starting to get a bit fed up. I snapped at Emma badly yesterday. The first week was all great, but now we've all spent too much time together. I'm very highly strung right now (understandably, I think) but she's been quite irritating and I ended up telling her as much. I don't feel bad. It actually felt good to speak my mind for once as I usually bite my tongue. I always reason that she's a teenager and I'm the adult so I have to be the mature one, but she can push my buttons. I guess the people closest to you can do that the most. I'm sure it's worse because I'm trying to stay all calm and relaxed and she's being a pain in the proverbial. Trying not to be stressed is stressful. She's going to Craig's granddad's farm on Monday for two nights, which will give us all a well-needed break, but today Craig's going to football in the car, so Emma and I are home together. I have no plans and am already dreading how to fill the day and put on a cheery face for Emma, when all I want is for the time to pass.

The only people who are available to do something at short notice are those with babies or children, and Craig doesn't want me to see them in case I get ill. I can't even go for a run or to the gym as it's not advised at this point. Argh, I need an outlet! It does make me grateful for my job. I'd go insane if I had this much free time all the time. I need stimulation, I need to use my brain and I need to exercise. I might slip out by myself, take a book and go get a coffee somewhere. That'll get me out for a bit and give me and Emma a bit of space from each other.

24 August 2015
Day 23

I went back to work today and I feel better for having a sense of purpose and something to occupy myself with. Saturday was rough. I felt irritable and tearful all day. Emma has gone to the farm now, so it was just me and Craig tonight, and we had a nice, peaceful evening. I'm so much more relaxed and comfortable when I don't have to put on a brave face for anyone.

I'm still having period pain quite a lot. I'm trying to work out if it's anything different from any other month, and I think it's probably a bit more than usual. It feels like it does the day before my period, rather than a week before. I can console myself with that – perhaps something is different. Although part of me is steeling myself for disappointment now. My mind is racing ahead to planning when we can try again and which deal to go for. I know I shouldn't, but I feel better when I know what my next move is. I shouldn't give up on the little embryos inside me though. For all I know, they're growing and thriving, while I've already written them off.

I said part of me was steeling myself for disappointment, but the other half is still hopeful and positive. Even though, as I'm writing this, I have such familiar period pain, I won't allow my thoughts to tell me that's definitely what it is. They're thoughts, not facts.

Earlier today, when I got in from work, Craig asked me to lie down with him on the bed. He never does that.

'Why?' I ask.

'Can't I give my pregnant wife a cuddle and make sure she's OK?'

I smile, despite wanting to tell him not to

say that, not to tempt fate.

'How are they doing?'

'I don't know,' I say, honestly.

'You keep growing in there,' he says to my belly, stroking it gently. I take his hand and squeezed it. He wants this as much as I do.

One week till test!

26 August 2015
Day 25

Five days until test. That's hardly any time, and yet also an eternity away. I've still got period pain. My belly looks bloated and swollen. It's rounded low down and does look a bit like a pregnancy bump. That makes me excited. I read today that it's common to be bloated and look pregnant days after conception, so I really could be! I've never seen my belly stick out like that in such a rounded shape before. It's definitely something different to normal. It could be a side effect of the medication, but I read the leaflet (at least six times) and it didn't mention bloating.

I'm feeling the period-like cramps now and tuning in to analyse if they are different. I think they might be more on one side, which could mean embryos implanting. Eek, I could be pregnant! I'm excited for test day, but also dreading it. I don't know how I'll dare do it. I might wee on myself.

27 August 2015
Day 26

Four days until test. I nearly can't bear it. I'd say I can't bear it, but I do bear it, because I don't have a choice. What would not bearing it look like? Crying hysterically? Losing my mind? Staying in bed all day? Well, I'm not doing any of those things, so I am bearing it.

I've still got my swollen belly and period-like cramps. Today I've also had a light pinkish beige discharge. At first I was pleased, thinking *implantation bleeding*, but now I'm worried it could be the start of my period, which is why I nearly can't bear it. It would be early for my period, but not unheard of.

Oh, and the other thing is, I have tingly nipples. Lots of things point to 'Yes', and today I'd almost convinced myself that I must be pregnant and I felt really happy, but now with the discharge and period-like feelings I don't know what to think. I wish I could stop thinking altogether.

We bought a First Response pregnancy test. It says you can do it up to six days before your period is due, so technically I could do it now, but I don't know if I dare. The clinic said not to test early, so that you're sure the result is accurate once you do it. It does say it's more accurate the closer you get, so perhaps we could hold out two more days and do it Saturday morning. Maybe I'll ring the clinic and ask if I'm allowed to do it early.

Oh, I nearly can't bear it. Argh!!!! Argh!!!! Bleugh, eurrrrr! I don't know what that is, I can't express it. Am I finally going insane?

Chapter 8
Licking our wounds

30 August 2015
Month 27

Sadly, it's a new month. My period arrived the day after I last wrote, I didn't make it to test day, which would have been tomorrow. The discharge continued the next morning when I was at work. I'd spoken to the clinic, and they'd said it'd be OK to do the test on the Saturday morning, so I was set to do that. Then at about 1 p.m. I went to the loo and saw dark blood. My heart froze and my stomach lurched sickeningly. I went all trembly. Luckily I was working from my local office, so I packed up my stuff and walked straight home without saying anything to anyone.

I logged on from home and carried on working as normal, which was a good distraction, but also OK if I fell apart, which was going to happen at some point. I got one of Emma's sanitary pads, as a tampon would mean admitting defeat, and I wasn't quite ready for that yet. There was part of me still hoping it was a heavy implantation bleed and there might still be a chance. I waited until Craig got in and told him I'd been bleeding but didn't know what it meant for sure. The bleeding got heavier throughout the evening and I knew it was my period. All of us were sitting in the living room watching TV and I had silent tears running down my face. Emma kept coming to sit by me and wanting me to play with her hair, but I couldn't face her and didn't know what to do, so I hid my face under a cushion, which was probably a bit of a weird thing to do. She thought I was playing around, but eventually Craig realised what was going on and came over to give me a cuddle. I was trying to cry quietly, but I felt awkward with Emma in the room so I went upstairs and let go. I cried the sort of tears you have when someone dies or you've had your heart broken. Real ugly face loud sobbing, the kind with snot everywhere and you can't catch your breath and think you might be sick. In a way it felt good to let myself feel that bad. I guess it was cathartic and partly relief that the very tense and difficult month was over. I eventually calmed down enough to speak.

'I'm sorry,' I say
'You've got nothing to be sorry for.'
'It's my body. I should have kept them alive.'
'You know it doesn't work like that. You couldn't have done anything.' I can see he was devastated, the light in his eyes dulled. 'Look, it would be amazing if we manage to have a baby together, but it's actually not the be all and end all. We'll be OK. We have each other, whatever happens.'
I can't say much to that. We have a long cuddle until the wretchedness eases a little.

I ended up going to sleep feeling calm,

then I did the pregnancy test on the Saturday morning, to be sure. The test confirmed it. I felt sort of resigned and OK. We got up early and did Park Run. It was good to be running again, but I got a rubbish time. Not that I'll beat myself up about that. Craig told me he had a little silent cry to himself while he was running round, which made me so sad, but also made me feel close to him. We're truly in this together, and I know that both individually and together we're strong. We can cope with this without it damaging our relationship.

Next, I had to let people know. I sent Cait a text. *'It didn't work, I'm not pregnant. Please don't ring just now. I'll be OK, just need some time.'* Her reply pinged back, but I couldn't face reading it straightaway.

Then I ring my mum. She's away for the weekend in Bournemouth and is in the middle of a busy market when she answers.

'Mum, it's me. I can't hear you, where are you?'

'Hang on, love, it's a bit noisy here. Let me find a quiet spot. OK, is that better? Can you hear me?' *lots of muffled noise*

'Yes, I can, just. It's not good news, but we're OK.' I start off bravely.

'OK, love.' Her tone tells me she knows it all, without me having to say anything else. Then I break down. There's no way I could give that news to my mum and not cry.

'It's OK, we'll be OK, we'll try again,' I keep insisting through sobs.

'I know you will, love. It's a good job you're so strong. I'm so proud of you, you know that, don't you?' Her voice is breaking too. And there we are. Two grown women sobbing down the phone, broken-hearted at the loss of the baby who wasn't to be.

This afternoon we went to Laura's to go for a walk. When I told her, she gave me a big cuddle. I cried again and she cried too, which I thought was nice. Then Craig came in and she brought him in too, like a three-way hug, then he filled up again as well. There's something moving about seeing a man cry. There's also something that feels good when things are really bad. It makes you realise how much your friends and family care about you and how lucky you are.

I might send out a text to everyone who knew about the IVF now, while I'm feeling brave, so that it's all taken care of and I can move on.

1 September 2015

It occurs to me that perhaps running a marathon together was preparation for this. The months of training, the commitment to the cause. The pure grit and determination needed to keep going on the day. Craig was there holding my hand when I hit the wall at seventeen miles and wanted to stay in the Portaloo. He smiled and held my hand. Together, we kept putting one foot in front of the other, through the pain, the weariness that makes you feel the floor is calling you to just lie down on it. The grey, continual downpour that you only get in Ireland. We eventually hobbled over the finishing line. I thought it was the hardest thing I'd ever do.

I was wrong.

This calls for a different kind of strength. Yes, the will to keep going, but someone keeps moving the finishing line. We must have passed the twenty-six mile mark by now. But we can't give up. What if we gave up the month before it was about to happen? You know where you are in the marathon: you can't give up now – you've just started, you're nearly halfway, you're past halfway, you've broken the back of it, only six miles to go, and so on. I have no idea where I am. Have I broken the back of it, or am I still on the first stretch and hideously underprepared? All we can do is hold hands and carry on.

Together.

We have a phone appointment with the doctor in a couple of weeks to have a debrief. They'll look at the medication and how I responded and they will talk about our options from here. I can't think straight to decide what those options might be. I might not write for a while. I'm too sad and I want to concentrate on normal living for now.

Chapter 9
One last push

5 October 2015
Month 28

I'm sitting at the edge of a frozen lake. It's not too bad here, there are lots of familiar things and the grass is quite comfy. I like the way the trees look against the blue sky, and there are sometimes rabbits, which are quite cute. But at the other side of the lake there's magic – unicorns and fairies – and there's also adventure – white water rafting, sky dives and giant rope swings in the trees (like Go Ape). It looks so much fun. It also looks a bit scary and hard, but I want to go there more than anything. To get there I'd have to walk across the frozen lake, and that means risking falling into the icy water. I fell in once before, not that long ago, and I've just got all dried and nice and warm again. Who knows how many more times I might have to get all cold and wet before reaching the promised land. I might never get there. Is it worth it? Should I set off again, or stay on this comfy grass with the trees and occasional rabbits?

These are the serious questions I've been asking myself. Am I prepared to put myself through more uncertainty, fear, hope and dread, and if so, how long for? Until I'm all-consumed by an obsession – until I no longer recognise myself because I've become damaged by icy water and have hypothermia?

OK, maybe I'm stretching the metaphor too far here. But I've been imagining how empowering it would be to step away, say, 'No thank you very much,' and get on with my life. I know, though, deep down, that it would be an escape route. It wouldn't be empowering, it'd be acting out of fear – fear that it wouldn't work and fear that I'd find trying again too much to bear. Acting out of fear doesn't lead to happiness – it leads to frustration, resentment and regret. It's better to act out of hope – hope that it will work. Then at least, if nothing else, I won't look back and think, 'What if?' For that reason – I'm in.

We're trying again. In two weeks' time, I start stabs round two.

11 October 2015

It's been a good break, doing normal not-trying-to-conceive-related things. We went to Copenhagen last weekend, just me and Craig, which was lovely. Had a great time seeing the sights and sampling the food and drinks. We've had nights out with friends and generally tried to enjoy ourselves. It did take a few weeks to feel normal again after the failed attempt. I was trying to be OK too soon and I just wasn't. You have to go through it, be patient and be kind to yourself. It takes time. I'm all good now, though, and it's been nice not to talk about it and not to think about it all the time.

Tip #10 Wallow, then stop wallowing

So, we're going ahead with the three attempts/refund programme. I start new stabs next Sunday. I don't want to egg share again, as we only ended up with three embryos and none of them reached blastocyst stage. I want to give us the best chance possible. It's a lot to hand over, but we're lucky enough to have the money saved up and not to have to get into debt. It's only money after all, not happiness. We can always earn more. It's totally worth it if we have a baby, and if we don't, we get most of the money back. We could then use it to go on the trip of a lifetime, lick our wounds and start our baby-free lifestyle. So all in all, I'm feeling OK now. The doc has given us a different medication to see if it works better for us. I start with Buserlin on cycle day 21 to suppress my normal cycle. That'll be 18 October, then I go in for a blood test on 30 October and, all being well, I start the Gonal F (the pen one I had before). Everything happens the same from then on. We're not taking time off work this time, apart from to attend appointments. I've told a couple of trusted people at work, so they're ready to cover for me as and when needed. My manager has been supportive, so that's made things easier. This time, I want to carry on as normally as possible. I don't want this to take over and become the focus of my life, like last time. I'm going to try to deal with it by not giving it too much of my energy and attention. I don't know how it'll go, but that's the plan at the moment.

I probably won't write as much, either. I

don't want to deliberate over every little thing, but I'll see how I feel. I do feel much calmer and as though I'll be able to take it in my stride (famous last words?!) Surely, having been through it once before, it won't be so scary at every step. I'm not worried about doing the injections now, and, by paying for three attempts upfront, we have backup if it doesn't work this time. We might need several attempts, so this is the next attempt – getting us closer to the one that works.

13 November 2015
Month 29

I've just read back through my last entry and am pleased to say everything has pretty much gone as I said. I've felt much, much calmer. In fact, for the first couple of weeks I was so busy at work, I hardly thought about it (seriously). It's coincided with one of the busiest times, where I organise a big event for 300 of the most senior bods. Previously I would have thought that would be a bad thing, but it's turned out to be a good thing. I've been doing injections in hotel rooms (including having to request a mini fridge for my room), in station toilets, on moving trains(!) – not ideal, but needs must.

So, we had our egg collection on Wednesday and we got nineteen eggs this time. Then we got the call yesterday to say fifteen of them have been fertilised – amazing! So, so different from last time. Perhaps my eggs don't hate Craig's sperm, after all.

It makes me think that if it doesn't work this time, out of that lot we're bound to have a few to freeze, and it will work eventually. Frozen transfers are much more straightforward, as well. There are no stabs, no egg collections. You go in at the right time of the month and they pop an embryo in.

We get a call tomorrow with a progress update, then, all being well, we go in for transfer on Monday. I'm feeling positive, so much more balanced and rational. One day at a time. I'm not trying to force or control things, I'm trusting and allowing things to follow their natural rhythm. (Philosophy classes have been totally worth it.) I'll write again when I have an update. Bye for now.

16 November 2015

Had the transfer today, one top quality embryo graded 5AA! That's the best you can get. Amazing! And as if that isn't enough, we have eleven in the freezer. Eleven! The staff at the clinic were impressed with our batch. They kept saying, 'Well done, guys,' as if it was down to our effort and hard work. We have a video of our embryo developing over the five days. It's pretty mind-blowing stuff. You see it as a fertilised egg – a circle with a dot in it – then it divides and becomes two circles, then four, then eight, then sixteen. Then it goes so fast you lose count. It triples in size, gets fuzzy edges, and a little sprout appears at the top left.

They said this is a good sign and it's ready to implant.

I completely over did the 'full bladder' in preparation for the transfer. They tell you to drink a pint of water an hour before – it's easier for them to get access to your womb if your bladder is full, because of the positioning of everything. Anyway, I had a cup of tea as well (and an orange juice). Then the appointment was running late. I literally have never needed a wee so bad. I thought I was going to burst. When I was on the bed I was actually shaking with the effort of not weeing myself.

The nurse told me to relax and I said, 'I'll wee on you if I do'.

She said, 'It's OK I've got my wellies on'.

As soon as they were done I leapt up. She said, 'You can pop behind the screen to put your clothes back on.'

I said, 'I can't,' and I ran across reception with a bare bum to get to the nearest loo (I kid you not). Luckily I had a long jumper on, so I could pull it down. The walk back from the loo was somewhat more embarrassing, but luckily there weren't many people about.

So out of the fifteen fertilised eggs, here's what we've now got:

5AA (in me)
5AB
4AA
4BA
4BA
4BA

4BA
4BA
3BB
3BB
3BB
2 (an early blastocyst)
morula
arrested
arrested

Arrested means they didn't carry on developing, not that they've been carted off by the police. Last time we had two morulas only. We're in another league!

23 November 2015

In the spirit of keeping busy during the two week wait, I roped Cait into coming away on a philosophy weekend with me. It was sold to us as a chance to relax, away from the hectic stresses and strains of everyday life, to do some yoga, go to some classes and eat some nice food. Sounded pretty good to me. It was at a lovely old manor house somewhere near Lincoln, so we had high expectations.

Well, I've never had such a bizarre experience in my whole life. We arrived about 9 p.m. on the Friday night and I was hoping to be shown where our room was, then to be offered a nice cup of tea and perhaps have a chat with some of the other people attending. We were ushered in through the door and told to leave our suitcases at the bottom of the stairs.

'The session has already started,' a

woman in her sixties, wearing a fluffy green jumper with an owl on it, told us.

'Oh well, that's OK, I guess we can take our stuff up to the room and –' I started.

She cut me off. 'This way.'

I glanced at Cait, who shrugged, so we followed. The woman took us down a corridor with creaky floorboards and oak panelling and ushered us into a room where five or six people were sitting in a semi-circle, listening to a woman at the front reading from a book. The woman was wearing slippers. We took our seats, mumbling our apologies for the disruption.

'There is no one hateful or dear to me. But those who worship me with love and devotion are very close to me, and I am also very close to them,' the slipper-wearing woman was saying. I caught Cait's eye and saw she was suppressing a smile. I felt my inner giggling schoolgirl threaten to surface, so quickly looked away, masking an involuntary snort with a throat clear. Had we accidentally joined a cult? I tried to look like there was nothing unusual going on as I took a sneaky peek at our companions for the weekend and wondered what had brought them here, and whether they were feeling vaguely ridiculous as well. There was a serious-looking man, I'd guess in his forties, wearing glasses. He appeared to be listening intently and he nodded sagely every so often. There was a plump-ish woman (also wearing slippers – we obviously missed that memo). She was fidgeting, crossing her legs this way then that and rearranging her hands in her lap. Ah, perhaps she's out of her comfort zone as well. Next were a youngish couple. I could tell they were a couple as their bodies were facing slightly towards each other, and every now and again one of them would lean over and whisper to the other, placing a hand on an arm or leg. I surreptitiously looked at my watch and wondered how long this session was going to go on for.

Eventually it drew to a close, and I was expecting to go and unpack and settle in, when it became clear this wasn't happening just yet. We were shown into a much bigger room with about a hundred people sitting theatre-style, with what I can only describe as some sort of 'leader' at the front. He gave off a definite preacher vibe. Then we *sang songs* with *no alcohol first.* Well, the others sang songs. It was all a bit much for me and Cait after a long drive and busy week at work. We sat there feeling a bit awkward and avoided eye contact lest our inner schoolgirls surfaced.

After the preaching/singing session was over, we spotted some print-outs of timetables for the weekend. To our distress, we saw that the following two days both started at 6. (a.m.) 6 a.m!! And didn't finish until 9 p.m. They included things like 'meditation', 'action in practice' (which we later learned was cleaning the bedrooms and bathrooms and/or helping prepare meals for a hundred residents) and there was an allocated slot for bath time. Erm? It felt like a peculiar boarding-school.

Needless to say, we didn't heed the 6 a.m. start time – I have an embryo to think about and need my rest – and we got told off. Told off!

Some of the philosophy sessions were OK. I went to a creative writing one, which is obviously quite up my street. Here's what I wrote:

Our instruction has been to 'write something' and that's it. My first thought was to write to my sprouting embryo, who I've lovingly nick-named 'sprouter', but I don't want to tempt fate, so I'm not doing that. It's quite strange here. The workshop next door is called 'Voice' and there's lots of chanting coming through the wall.

Being here sort of makes me wish I was at home having a 'normal' weekend, which would be staying in PJs late, cleaning the house, going for a run, reading, seeing family. But if I did the same thing every weekend, I'd stop appreciating it and get bored, which does sometimes happen. Part of the purpose of coming here was to relax and take my mind off the two week wait, which it definitely has done. I'm OK, in that respect, which is a huge change to last time I tried IVF. I said it's quite strange here. The oddest parts are probably the Sanskrit words used during pauses. Pauses are when we stop to take a breath between activities, which totally makes sense and I'm a fan of, but here, when they pause, they bow their heads and say – or more accurately chant – 'Ohm skaraduvu yedi' (or something like that). I definitely feel like I'm in a cult.

This morning we sang hymns, which I found odd. It's not a Christian weekend. I've always thought of philosophy as the opposite of religion – i.e. no dogma, with freedom of thought and challenge welcomed. Parts of this weekend fly in the face of that, which I can't quite get my head around.

Someone is shouting from next door in a very thespian way. It's quite amusing. I'm tired after the early start. Not quite as early as it was supposed to be, but early nonetheless. I feel like I've lost out on a weekend, but this one will stand out in my memory a lot more than lots of similar ones, so maybe I've actually gained something.

Interesting.

I'd like a curry. Random, but it just popped into my head. I quite like this exercise as it lets my mind go wherever it wants. I prefer that to trying to force myself to concentrate on what someone else wants me to listen to and discuss. Like this *morning's 'Devotion' session.*

Devotion is the theme of the weekend. I'm not sure about devotion, it feels too much like being devoted to a God. Anyway, curry, mmm. The food here has been really good – good as in nutritious for me and sprouter. Lots of fresh fruits, nuts and superfoods. Even Craig would be happy with the offerings, although they are all veggie, so perhaps he wouldn't.

This weekend is making me realise how much freedom I usually have and making me be grateful for it. My wrist is starting to ache from writing and I'm a bit conscious of the noise this pencil is making on the paper. Other people are using pens, and they make no noise. I hope we get a cup of tea after this. I'd like one. There's clinking outside the room. I'm hoping it's tea cups being set up. Gosh, I'm tired. I wonder what else I can write. It's nearly 4 p.m. I'm not sure what time this session finishes. I hope it's 4p.m. It looks like Cait is writing a poem. I wonder if she is. I'd like to read it.

Later in the evening, we were put into smaller groups to talk about 'how the weekend was going'. The talks were facilitated by the organisers and our teacher, Dave.

Organiser 1: 'So, how's everyone enjoying the weekend?'

'It's wonderful.'

Met with nods around the room and a raised eyebrow from me.

'I loved the 'voice' session. It really allowed me to reconnect with myself.'

I keep my expression neutral.

A woman sitting there quietly, twisting her hands in her lap is addressed directly.

'What did you think?'

'Erm, well it's good, it's just it's been more full on than I expected.' Brave woman.

'I was a bit surprised by the 6 a.m. start time.' I jump in to back her up.

'Some people ignored the start time.' Cait and I are given a pointed look from Dave, but I can see the hint of a smile playing on his lips.

'I had a busy week at work. I'm used to a lie-in at weekends,' I say, smiling back.

Organiser 2: 'It's important people participate fully. Let's be clear, the sessions are not optional.'

A sharp intake of breath from me. Dave looks uncomfortable.

Cait steps up. 'Sorry, I thought the whole weekend was optional.' (Said very politely.) Silent cheers from around the room.

It got a bit awkward and Cait and I decided we have to escape first thing in the morning. The very fact that we felt like it wasn't OK to leave made us dig our heels in and do it.

A low point of the weekend was during one particular 'action in practice'. We'd finished cleaning the showers and toilets (yep, really) and had to report back to the people handing out tasks. I was hoping they'd say, 'Well done, now go put your feet up until the next session,' but alas, they didn't. It was like we weren't allowed to have time off, unless the timetable said so. Instead, the organiser cast about for something for us to do and eventually sent us to the kitchen to 'reshape butter'. Is that even a thing? Apparently it is. The butters had been used at lunch and were no longer in their neat rectangle shapes. We had to make them into smaller rectangles by putting them in cling film and bashing them into shape. We did see a certain hilarity in this exercise.

The highlight of the weekend was the 'meditation walk'. We were allowed to do this independently, so Cait and a friend from our class and I wandered around the beautiful grounds of the building, sipping a sneaked bottle of Kopparberg cider in an act of rebellion. (Well, they sipped. I pretended because of my possibly pregnant state.) It was a bright, sunny winter's day with crispy frost on the grass and clear blue skies. We found a big swing hung from a tree and took it in turns to have a go. I felt calm and relaxed, happy even. To feel that way during an IVF two week wait is saying something. Have I developed the power of detachment? Would Swami Vivekananda be proud? Perhaps I have something to thank these philosophy bods for after all.

26 November 2015

It's the night before I can do the pregnancy test. My period is not here like it was last time and I've been 'relatively' calm. I've had a jam-packed itinerary to keep myself from dwelling as much as possible.

Today after work, Cait took me on a makeover and photoshoot. Not the sort of thing we'd usually do, but she had a voucher from somewhere and knew I needed entertaining. I stared at myself in the mirror after the girl had finished with me. I'd describe the look as 'caked'. I've never been a big make-up wearer, but come on – she'd made me look ten years older! The six layers of foundation were cracking around my eyes, magnifying any small wrinkles. My eyes were way too dark for my complexion and my eyelashes clumpy. (I'm very particular about my mascara.) I remembered why I insisted on doing my own make-up on my wedding day, much to the chagrin of some of my friends – 'But the photos!' I'd rather look like myself on the day, thank you very much. Anyway, I've digressed.

So, I'm staring at myself in the mirror.
'Do you like it?' the girl asks.
'Erm, it's a bit more than I'd usually wear.'
'Oh, well, let me see what I can do.' She grabs some cotton wool and starts dabbing at my cheeks. 'Better?'

It looks exactly the same. 'Sure, yes.' I smile. I'm only going home to wash it off and go to bed anyway.

We're waiting in the reception area for our slot with the photographer.

'I need a wee,' I say to Cait.

'The toilets are over there,' she nods in the direction.

'I know, but I can't look. What if my period has started while we're here? I'll cry all this make-up off and look like Courtney Love at her worst.'

'Oh. Well you can't not wee!'

It's OK, I've become adept at the closed-eye wee. Don't look. If you don't see it, it's not happening. Wee, wipe, flush. Only then can you open your eyes again. All good.

The photographer gets us doing some cheesy poses. Piggy-back anyone? I jump on Cait's back, I shouldn't be doing any heavy lifting, just in case. Then he asks us to lie down on our fronts and prop our make-up caked faces in our hands, feet kicked up at the back. Nice. When I lie on my front, my stomach feels achy and full. I'm bloated. I quickly squash any thought of wondering what that is. No wondering allowed.

So now I'm sitting in bed writing this. I haven't entertained the idea of doing the test early, because I can't bear the thought of getting a negative result, and then not knowing for sure if the negative result is because I tested too early. The test is sitting on the bathroom shelf, ready and waiting to tell me my fate first thing in the morning, and potentially change my life forever.

I can't allow myself to think too much. My coping strategy this time has been mainly to block it out and pretend it's not happening. I can't write much and I can barely think the thoughts. I don't want to bring them to the surface. All my hope and fear is nestled deep in the pit of my stomach. I'll go to bed tonight, squeeze Craig extra tight and do my best to ignore my somersaulting butterfly-infested insides. That's all I can say. I'm being as normal as possible.

Chapter 10
My happy ending

27 November 2015

I'M PREGNANT!!!!
Wow!!
Didn't know if I'd ever get the chance to write that. I've never felt so happy. I keep laughing and crying (happy tears obvs) then laughing again.

At 7 a.m. I could wait no longer. I'd been lying there for an hour, busting for a wee, stomach fluttering and heart beating a bit too fast. Feeling dizzy with the weight of the moment, I made my way to the bathroom and unwrapped the test with trembling fingers. Craig was with me. I planned to put the test to one side to wait for the recommended two minutes before looking, but as I went to put it on the shelf, a faint second line was emerging. I hardly dared breathe. I glanced at Craig. He'd seen it too and had a massive grin on his face. For the first time ever, I was holding a positive pregnancy test in my hand. He kissed me like he meant it, all the angst of the last two and half years slipping away and culminating in this moment. My trembling ramped up and I couldn't stop shaking, then the inevitable tears came, along with laughter. Once again I was a jibbering wreck, but this time an ecstatic, over the moon, gonna take off and fly sort of wreck. I then drank lots of water and did three more tests to be sure.

Our journey has made this all the more special and I'm not going to take any of it for granted. I'm going to enjoy every new experience it brings. I'm so excited for all of it. I'm excited about right now, I'm excited to get a bump, to have scans, to find out if it's a boy or girl, to feel the baby kick. I'm excited to feel sick and tired (if I do) and to give birth. I want to live it all and be awake and aware. Thank you so, so much Manchester Fertility, doctors, nurses, embryologists. Wow, wow, wow.

Epilogue

23 July 2016

I'll be thirty-nine weeks pregnant tomorrow. Only one week to go until my due date. I've been on maternity leave a week and it's pretty great so far. It feels a bit surreal to be writing this. I've flicked back, and this time last year we were gearing up to our first round of IVF. If I'd had a crystal ball and could see one year ahead I would have been extremely happy. I'm sitting in the sun, in the garden with a massive belly, feeling pretty much on cloud nine.

Being pregnant has been a blast. It's made all the waiting worthwhile. I haven't had any problems. I haven't really felt sick, aside from some mild queasiness early on. I've just enjoyed my growing bump. Perhaps it's some sort of karma – difficult conception = easy pregnancy. The best part is feeling her move. (Yes, we're having a girl.) Now she's big and can't change position much, I know which part of her is which. Her feet are tucked up under my ribcage on the right and her bum and back are to the left. Her head is low down in my pelvis, ready to come out.

I've swapped my TTC journal for a pregnancy journal, in which I write to my baby. I'm thinking of giving it to her when she's older. Here's an excerpt from earlier on:

Hello Lily, (we're pretty sure that's

*what we're going to call you)
I've suddenly got a lot bigger over the
last few weeks, which means you
have too. You kick me goodnight each
night and give me good morning
wiggles. You wiggle when I'm at my
desk at work and I'll stop what I'm
doing and sit there grinning, lovingly
stroking my bump, feeling like the
luckiest person in the world. Your dad
and big sister can feel you moving as
well when they put their hands on my
tummy. It's very special. Emma can't
wait to meet you. She's always
cuddling my tummy and talking to you.
She's wanted you a long time, too.*

*We went to Italy last week, so
you've already been to Rome and
Sorrento now, as well as Amsterdam.
You're quite well travelled already. I'll
show you the photos one day of
Mummy with a bump at the
Colosseum and in front of St Peter's
Basilica. The Italians love babies and
made a big fuss of me. They offered
me their seats on the bus – not in the
begrudging way they do at home, as
though they feel a bit awkward and
hope you'll say no so they can carry
on sitting – they actually stand up and
insist you sit down. It made me feel
very important and cared for. A couple
stopped their car to offer me a lift up a
hill from the beach (I politely declined)*

and a woman sitting opposite me on the train offered to share her food with me!

Since we got back, Grandpa has been over and painted a jungle scene on the wall of your nursery. It looks lovely. You'll know what I'm talking about as you'll have seen it every day when you read this.

I'm going to take a year off work to be with you and look after you. We're going to have so much fun together. We're going to do swimming lessons, baby massage, baby yoga. There'll be plenty of other babies for you to play with and get to know. It'll be our big adventure. Your first year in the world and my first year of being mummy to a baby. I can't wait.

Love Mummy x

'Oh, that'll be your waters,' Craig says, he passes me a towel as water gushes out of me movie-style and goes all over the carpet. It keeps coming, bucket loads of the stuff.

'What do we do?' I dance about on the spot. 'Shall I ring the hospital? Yes, I should ring the hospital, I'll do that.' I answer my own question. This was it!

'Hello, Maternity Assessment.'

'Hi, my waters have just gone. I'm forty weeks plus four days.'

'OK, we're actually closed at the moment.'

You're what? Hospitals don't close, plus you're answering the phone, so you're not closed.

'You can go to Dewsbury and someone will check it's your waters.'

'Erm, that's quite far away, and I'm pretty sure it's my waters.'

'Well, if you ring back in an hour, we'll see if we can fit you in then.'

'OK, I'll do that. Is it OK to go to sleep for an hour?' (It's bedtime!)

'Oh, just come straight in then. There might be a bit of a wait, but we'll see you. Bring a pad or towel with some of the waters on, so we can check it's amniotic fluid.'

I glance at the sodden towel on the floor. Really?

I get one of Emma's night-time maxi pads and get dressed. We gather our bags together calmly but with a growing sense of excitement and anticipation and set off, thinking we might be coming home with a baby.

When we get to the hospital, they're very busy, so there is indeed a bit of waiting around. They eventually check me over and confirm my waters have gone. (I wasn't in any doubt.)

'Have you had any contractions?' the midwife asks.

'No, I haven't felt anything.'

'OK, so you're not in labour. We can induce you, or you can wait twenty-four hours to see if it starts naturally.'

'I'll wait,' I say without hesitation. 'Can I

wait longer than twenty-four hours?' I really don't want to be induced.

'We don't recommend it. Once your waters break, you're at risk of infection. That protective bubble around the baby is gone.' I put my hands to my bump defensively.

'OK.' I pray for contractions to start. 'I've done hypnobirthing classes. Is there any chance I could be in labour and not know?'

She smiles indulgently. 'I'm sure the hypnobirthing classes will help you, but you'd definitely know.'

Fast forward two days and we had our baby. They stitched me up while I stared at her. They could have done anything just then and I wouldn't have cared. Craig was absolutely brilliant and although unfortunately my birth was long and traumatic, the end result was absolutely incredible. She was born at 10.33pm on 6 August 2016, forty-eight hours after my waters broke and three years, three months after we started trying to conceive. She weighed a healthy 7 pounds, 9 ounces and was the most perfect little human I've ever seen. That was when she chose to poo all over me.

I was elated, sitting there in hospital still pretty much covered in poo and blood, when Emma arrived to meet her sister. Her eyes were filled with so much love as she took in the sight of our tiny baby. She kissed us both, and straightaway both Mummy and big sister were sobbing with pure joy and incredulity that we'd reached this moment in time. Emma took Lily in her arms and I caught the look in Craig's eyes, seeing his two girls together. I told you right at the beginning I have a tendency to get a bit sentimental, so I'm going to wrap it up here. You get the picture – it was emotional and nice.

Fast forward two years and we have a rambunctious toddler who brings joy and chaos in abundance. Life is certainly not perfect and the last two years have come with their own challenges and of course, our story continues beyond our happy ending.

We're trying for another baby.

It's completely different and yet not different at all. We had a promising start, we got pregnant naturally, and really quickly too, but sadly it ended in miscarriage. Fertility problems are not any easier the second time around, and sometimes I feel like I'm right 'back there', but I know I can cope, as I coped before, and I believe we'll get there again.

As I write this, the memories of the difficulties of the birth have eased, and though I know it was traumatic, I now remember it fondly. Perhaps it's true that your brain blocks it out so you'll do it again, but I don't actually think so. I remember how it felt and the thoughts that went through my mind, but I also remember the bigger picture and the whole time around it. It was the most humbling, bewildering, wondrous and astonishing experience I've ever had the privilege of living through. If you're lucky enough to go through it, I hope you have the calm, serene birth experience I was hoping for. If not, take the drugs.

The difficult road to get pregnant the first time is still there, and those feelings have reared their heads again recently. But I take comfort in the fact that it was *worth it.* Totally and completely. I know some of you will be reading this thinking how lucky I am, and you're right. I'm lucky and so, so grateful. I won't take what I have for granted and the truth is, I wouldn't change what I went through to get here. I've always been an upbeat positive person and I believed that good things would happen to me in life, and generally they did. But it's easy to be upbeat and positive when things are going your way. When life throws you lemons, you're tested. Every experience in life is a lesson and after going through emotionally testing times you come out knowing yourself a little better and having more emotional resilience. That's when you really discover who you are. To misquote A.A Milne you find out, 'You're stronger than you thought, braver than you believed and happier than you knew.' Keep on keeping on, people. Your happy ever after, in whatever form it may take, is out there.

Tips for staying sane while trying to conceive

These tips are suggested with love. It's tough out there, and the truth is, there's no magic cure to make us feel better when we're in the thick of it. They won't all be for everyone, but if one or two of them help some of the people, some of the time, then I've achieved my aim.

Tip #1 Control your mind (or at least your thoughts)

Practise cognitively reappraising situations where the stakes are not as high as trying to conceive. For example, you might feel frustrated because your partner has finished off the milk and you want a cup of coffee. Perhaps they've done you a favour. You wanted to cut down on caffeine anyway, and didn't you buy that herbal tea to try, but hadn't quite got round to it? By starting off changing our thinking and reactions to simple every day niggles, it becomes easier to change our reactions to the big stuff. I didn't say easy, but *easier*.

Tip #2 Make a plan, but be prepared for it to change

Sometimes the hardest part of TTC is not being in control. If we can work out which elements we can control – if and when we decide to go to the doctor's for help, for example, or if and when we decide to have fertility treatment, and how to have fun in the meantime – it can ease that feeling of helplessness a little.

Tip #3 Look after your relationship

When I got married, one of our readings was 'The Art of a Good Marriage', by Wilfred Arlan Peterson. The line that stuck with me was, 'It's not only marrying the right partner, it is being the right partner'. It was a penny-dropping moment for me, as I'd always thought about finding the perfect person for me and not so much about what I brought to the party. Pretty shameful, if you think about it. So, make some deposits into that piggy bank, even if all you have the energy for is giving your partner an unexpected hug or making them a cup of tea. Making others happy makes us happy and you'll enrich your relationship, thus making things just a little bit easier.

Tip #4 Get a hobby

Sounds obvious and maybe a bit of an irritating suggestion. But it helped me. Aside from giving you something to do besides Googling fertility-related questions you already know the answer to, it gives you another aspect to your identity. You're not just someone struggling to conceive – you're also a philosophy student, an artist, a hockey player, dancer… (you get the idea).

Tip #5 Avoid getting hassle for not drinking

If you've decided to stop drinking completely, or to cut down, one of the most difficult/annoying things is having to explain yourself to others, without leading them to think you might be pregnant. Avoid putting yourself in situations where there's an expectation to drink, or, if you can't or don't want to avoid them, go armed with some techniques to keep your sobriety unnoticed.

Tip #6 Deal with envy/manage nosy friends and relatives

That friend of a friend who got pregnant on the first try? She married someone she doesn't love because she didn't think she'd find anyone else. They have nothing in common and he can't cook/doesn't do anything to help around the house/won't go out with her friends (substitute with something your partner is good at). Still want to swap places? Try it, it works. Managing nosy friends and relatives is just a matter of having some pre-prepared lines. You may have to say them through gritted teeth, but at least you won't be left floundering.

Tip #7 Get Russell in your life – or at least subscribe to his emails

Russell Davis of the Fertile Mind tells us our mind and body are one system. He believes our thinking and emotions can affect our bodies down to cellular level, which impacts on our chances of getting pregnant. Our minds affect our day-to-day experience of the journey, but they can also affect our ability to get pregnant, whether tying to conceive naturally or with fertility treatment.

Subscribe to Russell's emails for weekly wisdom and understanding.
http://thefertilemind.net/

Tip #8 Exercise

Do some exercise. Another tip that might sound annoying and might be met with eye-rolls. I get that, *but it really does work*! I won't bore you with science here – I'm sure you've heard it all before and you can do your own research. If you can make it part of your regular routine, all those endorphins will do wonders for your well-being.

Tip #9 Get enough sleep

Just this.

Tip #10 Wallow, then stop wallowing

It's OK to be sad. It's OK to cry, shout, stamp your feet and rage. In fact, it's a good thing. Do it. Own those emotions, then go and do something constructive or fun or self-indulgent, just for the hell of it.

Thanks and acknowledgements

My husband
For helping me to find the confidence to tell my story. For letting me share such intimate details of our lives when he is essentially a very private person, and for looking after the baby so I could write!

Saltaire Writers' Group
For welcoming me and offering encouragement on early drafts of this book.

Manchester Fertility
Aside from the obvious – for making my dreams come true, for reading, supporting and sharing my tale with your customers.

Russell Davis
For brightening up my darkest days with his weekly wisdom. And for letting me quote him.

School of Philosophy
For showing me another way of thinking about things, and for giving me some great material for my book!

My lovely beta readers
For reading early drafts and giving me invaluable feedback.

Rachel Cathan
Fellow fertility issues survivor and #indieauthor. For the support and advice along the way.

Jessica Hepburn
For being truly inspirational, I am in awe. I'm honoured that you read my book and gave me my cover quote.

Sam and Cristina @ Manufixed
For the complementary developmental edit which has shaped the final draft and improved my writing no end.

Helena Fairfax
My editor. For helping to shape the final cut and for teaching me the difference between a hyphen and an en dash. I love that geeky stuff.

Kerry Jordan
For lovingly designing my cover, it's perfect.

My friends
For their kind words and encouragement as I poured my heart and soul into this project.

My mum and dad
For 36 years of unwavering love and support and you know, for being my mum and dad.

My sister
For being an endless source of comfort and wisdom during my TTC years and for reading each draft of my book and saying just the right thing to help me on the way.

My big daughter

For being cool with being in this book. Love you.

My little daughter
For giving me my story to tell. For making my world a brighter place and filling my heart with joy, every day.

Thanks for reading, before you go - a favour; please post an honest review on Amazon or Goodreads to help others who may need it, find my book.

I love to hear from my readers, please stay in touch. You can follow me on Twitter @ToriDayWrites, check out my blog www.toridayblog.wordpress.com or email me at toriday@mail-me.com

Printed in Poland
by Amazon Fulfillment
Poland Sp. z o.o., Wrocław

66563882R00129